The Seven-Day -a- Week Church

The Seven-Day -a- Week Church

Lyle E. Schaller

Abingdon Press
Nashville

The Seven-Day-A-Week Church

Copyright © 1992 by Abingdon Press

This book is printed on recycled, acid-free paper.

Library of Congress Cataloging-in-Publication Data

Schaller, Lyle E.
  The seven-day-a-week church / Lyle E. Schaller.
    p.   cm.
  ISBN 0-687-38144-4 (alk. paper)
  1. Big churches. I. Title. II. Title: 7-day-a-week church.
BV637.9.S33   1992
254—dc20   91-31287
                                                                        CIP

MANUFACTURED IN THE UNITED STATES OF AMERICA

To
Bob Buford
Fred Smith

CONTENTS

CHAPTER FOUR

Staffing the Full-Service Church

93

CHAPTER FIVE

Who Runs That Big Church?

115

CHAPTER SIX

Continuity and Succession

137

CHAPTER SEVEN

Clouds and Questions

149

NOTES

INTRODUCTION

The origins of this volume can be traced back several years to the urgings of friends to write a book on the life and ministry of the very large church. Many of those doing the urging were pastors, staff, and volunteer leaders I met while engaged in three- to five-day parish consultations with very large churches. Others were participants in seminars and workshops designed for leaders from very large congregations.

While I worked on a tentative outline and the contents, a half-dozen discoveries grabbed my attention and redefined the project. The first was the gradual recognition back in the late 1970s that churchgoers born after World War II were showing up in disproportionately large numbers in large and rapidly growing churches—especially in relatively new congregations—that either did not carry a denominational label or wore it very lightly with low visibility. This, of course, is now widely recognized as one of the reasons several of the mainline Protestant denominations report that their members are growing fewer in numbers and older in age. These denominations cut back sharply during the 1960s and 1970s in the launching of new missions—and especially in new congregations designed to grow into megachurches.[1]

The second discovery was the simplest and most obvious. It is impossible to offer generalizations that apply to every state and province in the United States and Canada. While the Sunday morning churches described in chapter 2 are shrinking in number—especially in the Northeast, the Midwest, the Great Plains, and the far West—many continue to thrive in retirement communities in the Sunbelt and in the theologically more conservative sections of the Southeastern United States and in communities that attract large numbers of weekend tourists.

The third discovery was the reluctant realization that the larger the size of the congregation, the more likely the continuity, creativity, and vision rest in the staff, not in the volunteer leadership. By contrast, the continuity in the typical small congregation rests largely in the institutional culture rather than in the paid staff. As a denominationalist and as a product of the 1950s—which taught that people's loyalties should be to Jesus Christ, the church, and the denomination, not to one particular congregation—I found that this was a bitter pill to swallow. The acceptance of that new reality, however, does help to explain a significant part of contemporary church life. It is one of the three or four most plausible explanations for the decrease in the number of United Methodist congregations averaging more than 350 at worship from over 2,000 in 1965 to fewer than 1,300 in 1990. This also helps to explain the institutional fragility of the very large Sunday morning church built around the personality and preaching of the senior pastor, which is described in chapters 2 and 6. This recognition of the centrality of the leadership role of the pastor and program staff also helps to explain the rapid growth of Protestant churches in Korea[2] as well as of the large independent churches in the United States that cannot depend on a denominational label to attract new members.

The fourth and most intriguing of these six discoveries was the sudden realization one day back in 1988 that the category I had identified simply as "the very large church" really was a combination of two groups of large congregations. The first, which has become an endangered species, is the Sunday morning church described in chapter 2. The second group, which is increasing in numbers, is the large and rapidly growing parish that offers an expanding seven-day-a-week program. Some of these programs are clearly community outreach or social service-type ministries, directed largely at people who never will become members. Most of these weekday and evening ministries, however, also represent attractive entry points for potential future members. The most obvious result of that insight was a change in the theme of this book from "The Life and Ministry of the Very Large Church" to its present title.

The fifth discovery occurred during a three-cornered literary debate that began back in the 1970s. This debate was begun by scholars in the

Church Growth Movement who pointed out that numerically growing congregations usually attract new members who closely resemble the current members. This pattern was identified as the "homogeneous unit principle."[3] The accuracy of this generalization rarely was challenged.

Subsequently, however, a growing number of critics of the Church Growth Movement challenged the homogeneous unit principle on ideological grounds. They argued that every congregation should be inclusive. Every congregation should plan to attract and serve every slice of the population. Targeting one group of people as prospective new members sometimes was described as "exclusionary" or even as "unchristian." At a minimum it was ideologically unacceptable.

Rarely did anyone point out that the congregations most likely to reflect the homogeneous unit principle were not the numerically growing churches, but rather the declining congregations affiliated with one of the "mainline" Protestant denominations.

From the third corner of this debate came two reservations. First was the qualification offered by the pragmatists that a more precise statement would read, "Numerically growing congregations naturally tend to reflect the homogeneous unit principle *unless a carefully managed effort is made to build in a greater degree of pluralism.*" The second qualification occurred to this observer in June 1984 when I began to realize the best examples of carefully managed pluralism that violated the homogeneous unit principle could be found in that growing number of full-service congregations that included a large core of working class adults, their adult children, and other adults from their children's generation.

This expression of pluralism can be found in the large seven-day-a-week African-American churches, in the large working class immigrant congregations with a seven-day-a-week program as well as in the large and vital ethnically integrated full-service churches and the largely Anglo program churches.

Those who examined every congregation from the perspective of the homogeneous unit principle argued that this oversimplified reality. Most of the people in these large, growing, and vital seven-day-a-week churches shared a single characteristic. This meant they really reflected the homogeneous unit principle. That widely shared single characteristic was not race or income or language or nationality or age or education or social class. It was a desire for upward mobility for themselves and/or their children.[4]

A more careful analysis revealed that for many of these large and rapidly growing megachurches that single-factor explanation of upward mobility also oversimplified reality. The real point of homogeneity for many (but not all) of these large and rapidly growing full-service churches can be summarized in four sentences.

1. The people worshiping in these churches discover that their lives have been transformed by the power of the Gospel.
2. That happens because the leaders (both paid and volunteer) have experienced the transformational power of the gospel in their own lives; therefore, they are convinced that they must share that experience with others.
3. Most of the members cannot help inviting others to come and experience the transformational power of the Good News about Jesus Christ.
4. As a result, these churches operate on the assumption that more people will come if invited by those whose lives have been transformed by the gospel. Thus a self-perpetuating cycle is created that generates a steady flow of visitors. As is pointed out in chapter 2, while this is not the only reason these churches often become very large, it is the number-one factor.

The last, the most recent, and the happiest of these six foundational discoveries I owe largely to Robert Buford, W. Fred Smith, and *The Leadership Network*.[5] Many old men are tempted to romanticize the past, to glorify the heroic figures of an earlier era, and to bemoan the contemporary absence of outstanding leaders, preachers, tenors, scholars, lefthanded baseball pitchers, and honest politicians. To offset that predictable tendency, I have been honored to have had the opportunity to meet and talk with scores of senior pastors, associate ministers, and executive pastors born since 1950 who are among the most competent leaders I have ever known. As a group they are highly committed, bright, optimistic, skilled, Christ-centered, enthusiastic, goal-driven, compassionate, visionary, intelligent, caring, and entrepreneurial leaders. They have been willing to accept and to fulfill the responsibilities of serving as initiating leaders. They are highly productive workers who know how to get the most out of each hour God has given them. They reinforce the conviction that God does lift up the leaders needed for each new generation. The only point of concern is whether the supply will be adequate to meet the growing need.

The product of those six discoveries is this book. This is not simply a book about that rapidly growing number of very large program churches. Rather this book is about yesterday and tomorrow.

The big Protestant churches of the 1950s were built largely around the ecclesiastical trinity of that day—inspiring preaching, a superb choir, and an attractive Sunday school. For all practical purposes, these were Sunday morning churches. That mixture often was enriched by Sunday evening services and the personable—and sometimes controversial— long-tenured senior minister who also often earned a role as a respected community leader.

The big Protestant church of.today and tomorrow also is built around worship and memorable preaching, but that superb choir is only one component of an extensive ministry of music; the Sunday school is but one component of a huge teaching ministry; and the schedule is filled with a variety of other events, classes, programs, and groups. These are the seven-day-a-week churches that are emerging as the successors to the big Sunday morning churches of the 1950s. The mixture of characteristics that are a part of the culture of these program churches often is enriched by a senior minister who is an initiating leader and who has brought together a collection of energetic, creative, daring, imaginative, productive, committed, venturesome, and personable individuals to serve as the program staff.

When the scholars of the middle third of the twenty-first century review the recent history of the Christian churches, they will lift up several changes that can be dated in the second half of the twentieth century. At or near the top of that list will be the rapid growth of Christianity in Africa and the phenomenal growth of Pentecostalism in South America. Also high on that list will be the beginning of the post-denominational era, which has created a supportive context for the rapid increase in the number of large seven-day-a-week churches.[6] From today's perspective, the emergence of the seven-day-a-week church as the successor to the big Sunday morning churches of the 1950s is one of the most significant developments of this century.

Much of the discussion in this book contrasts two types of Protestant churches. One is the traditional congregation that has concentrated most of the structured or scheduled programing on Sunday morning. The second is the parish that has created an extensive seven-day-a-week ministry with only a minority of the events, activities, programs, gatherings, services, groups, and classes scheduled for Sunday morning. In order to facilitate the flow of the book, two synonyms are used repeatedly for that more awkward term *seven-day-a-week church*. One is the "program church." The other is the "full-service church." While a few may quarrel with this, in this volume all three carry the same meaning.

Finally, contemporary standards requiring full disclosure make it advisable to warn the reader that for all but three out of the past thirty-two years this writer has been on the payroll of a parachurch organization. The first eight of those years were spent as Director of the Regional Church Planning Office, which was created, owned, and financed by fourteen Protestant denominations in northeastern Ohio. That was followed by three years at Evangelical Theological Seminary. I have spent the past twenty-one years as the Parish Consultant on the staff of the Yokefellow Institute, a parachurch organization with headquarters in Richmond, Indiana. These experiences obviously colored the perspective for the writing of the first chapter of this book. Absence of a denominational label on my employer's headquarters also has made it easier for me to work with pastors, volunteer leaders, and officials from five dozen different religious traditions during the past three decades as well as with leaders from scores of large, nondenominational, or independent, full-service churches.

I am indebted to all of them for their candor, comments, cooperation, corrections, courtesies, criticisms, ideas, insights, observations, patience, questions, reflections, suggestions, and thoughtfulness.

CHAPTER ONE

The Changing Face of American Christianity

For one hundred and seventy-five years the Congregationalists and the Anglicans dominated the church scene in the American Colonies. In 1780, in the middle of the Revolutionary War, these two denominations reported a combined total of 1,155 congregations. That was nearly one-half of the 2,331 churches in the Colonies in that year.

Forty years later, in 1820, the Baptists and the Methodists each reported approximately 2,700 congregations. The Presbyterians were third with 1,700 congregations, followed by the Congregationalists (1,100), the Lutherans (800), the Episcopalians (600), and the Quakers (350).[1] In only four decades the face of American Christianity had been transformed.

An equally radical change has been occurring during the past four decades with the emergence of what some observers have labeled "the post-denominational age."[2] Whether denominationalism is dying is a question outside the scope of this book. What is clear, however, is that many of the duties and responsibilities that once had been fulfilled by denominational agencies are now being carried by new players on the scene.

These changes also have provided a hospitable environment for the emergence of the very large full-service Protestant churches that operate a seven-day-a-week ministry. A brief review of a few of these changes may help to explain the contemporary rapid increase in the number of these large-program churches as well as their special attraction to the generations born after World War II.

As recently as 1955 the predecessors of what today are eleven predominantly Anglo religious traditions plus five large African-American denominations dominated American Protestantism.*

The Roman Catholic Church in the United States was a completely separate religious tradition and only rarely did Catholics and Protestants cooperate on issues of common interest. One of the few points of contact was the occasional interfaith marriage—and in three out of four, that couple ended up in the Catholic Church.[3]

During the early part of the 1950s these denominations provided most of the preachers for religious services that were carried over the radio or television. Public officials usually turned to a church affiliated with one of these denominations when they sought a Protestant minister to invoke God's blessing on a civic event. Congregations usually turned to their denominational headquarters when they ordered Sunday school materials or when they needed advice on improving the Christian education program. The youth attended a summer church camp owned and operated by a regional judicatory of that denomination.

If the pastor possessed a seminary degree, that usually meant he had graduated from a seminary affiliated with one of these denominations. If and when he took time off for continuing education, it usually was at an event sponsored by that denomination. The missionary supported by that congregation usually was a member of that denomination and had been sent to the field by that denomination. Only rarely did a congregation seeking a new minister go outside their own denominational family.

The overwhelming majority of new Protestant churches organized during the early and mid-1950s were launched under a denominational flag with a denominational blessing. Three out of four members who transferred their membership from one congregation to another continued within that same denominational family. Three out of four adult members of these dominant denominations were second or third generation members of that particular religious tradition.[4]

*These sixteen denominations or traditions are the Southern Baptist Convention; The United Methodist Church; the Evangelical Lutheran Church in America; The National Baptist Convention, U.S.A., Inc.; The Presbyterian Church (USA); The National Baptist Convention of America; The Lutheran Church—Missouri Synod; The Episcopal Church; The African Methodist Episcopal Church; The Assemblies of God; The United Church of Christ; American Baptist Churches in the U.S.A.; The African Methodist Episcopal Church Zion; The Christian Church (Disciples of Christ); The Church of God in Christ; and The Churches of Christ.

The Sunday school classes and adult study groups of that era usually turned to their own denominational publishing houses for their curriculum materials. The hymnal in the pew rack was published by that denomination. Many of the books and magazines in the pastor's library were published by that denomination, as were the bulletin covers used for worship. If a congregation needed outside help on a capital funds campaign or advice on expanding their physical facilities, they usually called on a denominational staff person. The format for youth ministries usually was one designed by denominational leaders, and the youth group carried a denominational name. The women's organizations usually functioned in a structure designed by denominational leaders, and their central reason for being was to support the denominational missionary program.

If and when the pastor and a group of volunteer leaders spent a day or two or three at a church meeting, that usually was either the annual convention of the regional judicatory of that denomination or at an event sponsored by the parent denomination.

When a committed young man told his pastor that he felt a call to go into the full-time Christian ministry, the pastor not only encouraged him, but also strongly recommended a seminary affiliated with that denomination.

When one of the core families moved to another state, it was taken for granted that they would seek out a new church home from within that same denomination. It was not uncommon in several denominations for the pastor to recommend a specific congregation and to write that minister to be sure to contact this family immediately after their arrival.

Most of the adult leaders in these churches back in the early 1950s were born between 1875 and 1925. Most of them appeared to be comfortable in what was essentially a closed denominational system. The expansion of these closed denominational systems both created and was encouraged by the need for an unprecedented increase in the number of the professional staff in both national and regional judicatory offices.

Most of those closed denominational systems of the 1950s broke open during the last half of the twentieth century. Why?

Why Did They Open?

The number-one reason, of course, was that most of those leaders of 1950, both lay and clergy, died or retired. The second most powerful force for change was that their children did not inherit that preference for closed institutional systems. Scores of other reasons could be identified, such as the impact of the Second Vatican Council on the Roman Catholic Church in America.[5] Today the number of people leaving a Roman Catholic parish for a Protestant church greatly exceeds the number going the other direction.[6] At least six and perhaps as many as thirteen million Americans reared in Roman Catholic homes and parishes are now regular worshipers in Protestant churches.

Another influential, but largely ignored, change came in 1960. In that year the Federal Communications Commission ruled that local radio and television stations could sell air time for religious programming and still get credit for "public service" for those hours. Up until 1960 the "sustaining" time for religious programming was free and was filled largely by churches and ministers affiliated with the dominant religious traditions. Those outside the mainline traditions had to pay for most of their air time. Relatively few of the mainline Protestant or Catholic or Jewish leaders were willing to pay the new charges.[7] The independents had been paying and continued to do so. One result was that religious programming carried over radio and television became a near monopoly of the independent and evangelical religious traditions, while the mainline denominations forfeited much of their earlier visibility. Another result was that senior ministers of the very large congregations have replaced denominational leaders as the public image of American Protestantism on radio and television.

Among the many other factors behind the opening of what had been largely closed denominational systems are (1) the erosion of denominational and other institutional loyalties among the generations born after 1940; (2) the emergence of dozens of "transdenominational" seminaries that began to compete with the historic seminaries for students; (3) the impact of denominational mergers in eroding institutional loyalties; (4) the disappearance of the geographical or "neighborhood church" as people who commute five to forty miles to work find it easy to commute five or ten or twenty miles to church; (5) the improvement in the quality and safety of urban and suburban highways; (6) the expectation by many that a convenient off-street parking space will be available at the end of the journey; (7) the growing demand for higher-quality physical facilities (church basements are far less popular with people born after 1955 than they were with those born before 1925), preaching, music, nurseries, teaching, and youth ministries; (8) the recent rapid increase in the exodus of people born since 1945 from Roman Catholic churches into evangelical and charismatic Protestant congregations; (9) the simple fact that most Americans born after 1940 grew up in a world of big institutions, including public schools, employers, shopping malls, universities, and medical clinics; (10) the capability of large churches to design and staff a huge range of specialized ministries; (11) the power of the critical mass—the twenty-six-year-old, never-married adult looking for a spouse is more likely to be successful in that search in a singles ministry that includes 1,200 people than in a group of nine singles; (12) the shift in priorities in many long-established congregations and denominations from people and their needs to institutions and the priorities of the denomination; (13) the focus on attendance in megachurches contrasted with an emphasis on membership in the long-established congregations (in scores of megachurches the average worship attendance is double or triple the membership total, while in some long-established smaller churches the membership total may be double the worship attendance); (14) a more persuasive public-relations and advertising program in megachurches than in smaller congregations (see chap. 3); (15) a sensitivity and responsiveness to "the market" as opposed to smaller congregations being driven by tradition; (16) the refusal by an increasing number of municipalities to grant permission to long-established congregations to increase their off-street parking or to expand their physical facilities because of complaints from the neighbors; (17) the decision by a growing proportion of that group of three to seven million Americans who have been attending two churches every week in order to have their religious needs met to switch to "one-stop shopping" at a megachurch; (18) the search by millions of people born in the 1942–67 era for a Christ-centered church that offers Bible-centered preaching and teaching ministries; (19) the capability of the larger churches to offer a broad range of choices, not only in the times for worship, but also in how they can be engaged in doing ministry—the seven-day-a-week program churches use a smaller proportion of volunteers' time and energy in maintaining the institution; (20) the inability of the vast majority of Protestant churches in the late 1960s to welcome the Jesus People, many of whom helped form the nucleus for what subsequently became a large, full-service congregation; (21) a greater preference for a faster pace for corporate worship; (22) the shift toward the theological left by many pastors, while most of the churchgoers born since 1955 are theologically more conservative than their parents; (23) the satisfaction gained by members when they learn that 20 to 35 percent of their contributions are allocated to missions, benevolences, and community outreach compared to the 10 to 16 percent that is typical of smaller congregations; (24) the tremendous increase in the number of people who eat breakfast out of the home, including those who eat breakfast at church; (25) the inability or unwillingness of the vast majority of long-established churches to accommodate that growing number of self-identified charismatic Christians who seek a church with a prayer-and-praise service; (26) the impact on evangelical and independent churches of the insights gained and shared by the Church Growth Movement;[8] (27) the decision by several mainline denominations to cut back sharply in new church development in the 1960s and 1970s; (28) the impact of television and public address systems on preaching styles and public discourse; and (29) while rarely mentioned, this may be among the top half-dozen factors, the emergence of a huge generation of gifted, energetic, committed, creative, visionary, Christ-centered, venturesome, self-confident, and entrepreneurial pastors born after World War II who prefer the open ecclesiastical system over a closed system.

Is Competition the New Variable?

If a man can write a better book, preach a better sermon, or make a better mousetrap than his neighbor, though he builds his house in the woods the world will make a beaten path to his door. (Ralph Waldo Emerson)

Economic determinists and those who believe in the power of the marketplace may agree that Emerson had a point. The attractiveness of a better quality product has replaced inherited loyalties, geographical convenience, and denominational allegiance in changing the face of American Christianity during the past four or five decades. This point of view can be summarized in one word: *competition*.

That one word is a big part of the explanation behind the sponsorship of contemporary religious programming on radio and television. That one word also explains why the majority of long-established small Protestant congregations are shrinking in numbers. Most do not have the range of resources necessary to attract new generations of churchgoers. That one word also summarizes the current state of affairs as theological seminaries seek registrants for the next fall's entering class. That one word is far more influential than the location of the meeting place in explaining why this three-year-old new mission averages well over four hundred at worship while that one averages fewer than one hundred. That one word, along with the increase in interdenominational marriages, helps to explain the rapid growth in the proportion of newcomers to a community who "shop" three or four or more congregations from various denominations before deciding on a new church home.

That one word explains why scores of "old First Church downtown" congregations are larger, stronger, and more vital today than ever before in their history while many others are well past the halfway point on the road to dissolution.[9] That one word also is a big part of the explanation for the emergence of the seven-day-a-week program churches or what Peter Drucker identifies as "pastoral" congregations.[10] That one word also helps to explain the numerical growth of several branches of American Protestantism, while other branches report continuing numerical decline.

That one word also helps to explain many of the pressures for reform in the public schools, the creation of hundreds of new private Christian day schools, the recent phenomenal growth of the home schooling movement, and the centrality of children's ministries in many seven-day-a-week churches.

The increase in competition among the churches for new members, for staff, for the allegiance of people, and for other resources is a significant part of the contemporary ecclesiastical context. The emergence of a more competitive context certainly is a big factor behind the recent increase in the number of very large congregations. Competition certainly is a significant part of the context that has encouraged the rapid growth of the large-program churches.

References to the power of the marketplace and the increase in competition, however, do tend to oversimplify what has been happening. To see the larger picture, it is necessary to look at the rapid growth of parachurch organizations in recent decades.

Who Created the Competition?

The description offered in the early pages of this chapter of the ecclesiastical scene of the early 1950s is accurate, but it is not a complete picture. One omission is that while they had low visibility at the time, several relatively new religious traditions were experiencing remarkably rapid numerical growth. The Churches of Christ, the Church of the

Nazarene, The Assemblies of God, the Mormons, the Seventh Day Adventists, the Conservative Baptist Association, and others represented one source of competition. Another was the growing number of independent or nondenominational congregations that have emerged during the past four decades.

The big omission, however, from that earlier description was the emergence and growth of parachurch organizations. Some date their beginnings back several decades or more, but most came into existence after 1940. One of the first cracks in that closed denominational system appeared with the growing array of parachurch organizations created to minister to college and university students. A second, and somewhat smaller exception was the parachurch organizations seeking to reach and serve high school students. The third was that growing number of parachurch organizations designed to engage adults in extended and serious study of the Holy Scriptures. A fourth was that huge variety of nondenominational evangelistic ministries that utilized tents, radio, vacant theaters, and, later, television, to preach to whomever might watch or listen. A fifth included that huge variety of parachurch organizations created by entrepreneurs to expand the range of choices in Christian education materials, music, books, filmstrips, and Christian magazines.[11]

The lines were drawn rather clearly, however, as regional and national denominational agencies serviced congregations while the parachurch organizations concentrated on reaching individuals. (It may not be an irrelevant coincidence that the new parachurch organizations in Korea in the 1960s provided specialized ministries to individuals such as chauffeurs, garbage workers, students, athletes, barbers, entertainers, factory workers, clinical patients, and prisoners. More recently, Korean parachurch groups have expanded their focus.)

The late 1950s and the 1960s brought a new entry to that ecclesiastical landscape marked by the word *cooperation*. From the perspective of leaders in the mainline denominations this included an expansion of the program departments in the National Council of Churches, the creation of new departments in state and metropolitan councils of churches, and the organization of ad hoc interdenominational agencies on planning, pastoral counseling, continuing education, race relations, anti-poverty programs, peace, social justice, feminism, housing, social welfare programs, and other issue-centered ministries. In many of these an important partner was the Federal government, which partially funded cooperative efforts in housing, Head Start programs, and a remarkable array of social welfare ministries.

From a congregational perspective this era marked the beginning of a new relationship between many parachurch organizations and local churches. One by one, parachurch organizations began to shift their focus from individuals to congregations. For a few, the congregation became the number-one client. In other settings the parachurch organization saw itself as a partner with one or more congregations in youth ministries or in renovating vacant housing units or in attacking the policies of City Hall or in seeking to alleviate world hunger or in recruiting and supporting missionaries in the Third World or in ministering to single adults or in establishing a community pastoral counseling center or in supporting a retreat center or in staffing a food pantry.

The clearest measurable dimension of this cooperative arrangement between congregations and parachurch organizations could be found in congregational budgets. Back in the 1950s nearly all of the benevolence items in the typical denominationally affiliated church were sent through denominational channels. Three or four decades later it was not uncommon to find that one-fourth to two-thirds of one congregation's benevolent contributions were designated for parachurch organizations.

The Contemporary Scene

The post-1980 era has been marked by continued growth in the number and variety of parachurch organizations. This has been paralleled by a cutback in the number of program staff in most of the mainline Protestant denominations and in councils of churches. That may not be a coincidence.

More significant, however, has been the expansion of the clientele of the parachurch organizations. Thirty-five years ago most parachurch organizations serviced individuals. That is still true for some, except that the numbers have grown. However, at least three dozen of the growing parachurch organizations are now concentrating their resources on servicing congregations. Gradually they are now offering services that formerly were provided by regional and/or national denominational agencies.

People of the 1700s and 1800s might have protested that this is not a new trend. They could point to earlier parachurch organizations, such as the American Home Missonary Society (1826), the American Board for Foreign Missions (1810), the American Sunday School Union (1824), the American Bible Society (1816), the American Peace Society (1828), the American Tract Society (1825), The American Society for the Colonization of the Free People of Color of the United States (1816), the American Anti-Slavery Society (1833), and the National Women's Christian Temperance Union (1874), to prove their point.

Most of these organizations were established as movements to promote a cause. By contrast, most of the contemporary parachurch organizations have been organized to bring the gospel to groups of people not reached by the churches and/or to create and staff specialized programming such as Bible study, evangelism, youth ministries, training caregivers, or continuing education. They have been created to do what the denominations have not been doing or to service a clientele largely overlooked by denominational programming.

The Expanding Role of Theological Seminaries

Concurrent with this increase in the number and variety of parachurch organizations came an expansion in the outreach of scores of theological seminaries. The largest and most visible components of this were the one-week or two-week continuing education programs for pastors and the offering of the Doctor of Ministry degree. In addition, several seminaries offer extensive programs for the training of lay-program specialists and seminars for denominational executives and for those engaged in specialized ministries.

A growing number of seminaries now include a center or department that provides consultation services to parishes. A few are producing printed or videotape or audiotape curriculum resources. The seminaries also are beginning to see congregations as one of their clients. In addition, a few are servicing denominational headquarters staff. It is too early, however, to predict the role of theological seminaries in American Protestantism in the year 2015. Several are faced with more pressing problems, including the competition for the most promising candidates,[12] expanding budgets, a tight placement market for their graduates, and the decision by many large program churches to look elsewhere for staff.

Perhaps the most interesting facet of this evolutionary pattern is the increasing number of denominational agencies, both regional and national, that are contracting with parachurch organizations or with theological seminaries to do what in 1960 would have been done by denominational staff or by staff from a council of churches. Examples include capital fund campaigns, church-growth programs, continuing education events for both laity and clergy, publications, Bible study resources, parish consultations, training ministers to plant new churches, studies for organizational restructuring, initiating new ministries, films, specialized training events for leaders from large churches, videotapes, and adjunct or temporary program staff for a particular parish.

What denominational agencies once did for themselves they now are asking parachurch organizations to do. In quantitative terms, the cutbacks in the number of denominational program staff have been more than offset by the increase in the staff of parachurch organizations.

In recent years a new variation of the parachurch organization has surfaced. The independent, self-governing groups that relate largely or entirely to a single denomination but exist outside that denomination's structure. For many years the Presbyterian brands were recognized by the Presbyterian Church (U.S.A.) as "Chapter 9" organizations. They could carry the word *Presbyterian* in their name, but they were outside the control of the General Assembly.

Other examples of parachurch organizations identified with one denomination include the Baptist Cooperative Missions Program, Inc., Episcopal Renewal Ministries, the Biblical Witness Fellowship (UCC), Presbyterians for Renewal (PCUSA), International Lutheran Renewal Center, The Mission Society for United Methodists, and Disciple Renewal. It is far too early to predict the role of these and similar parachurch groups in the years ahead.

A New Player in the Game

While it resembles the chicken-and-the-egg argument, it is clear that as denominational agencies and councils of churches cut back on servicing congregations, the parachurch organizations move in to fill that vacuum, occasionally as a goad to denominations, but far more often with new programs in response to new needs.

Today, however, the choices for most Protestant churches no longer are limited to denominational headquarters or to a theological seminary or a parachurch organization. A new player has entered the game. This is the large, full-service congregation, or the megachurch.

Between 1950 and 1990 the number of Protestant congregations averaging eight hundred or more at worship has at least tripled and perhaps quintupled. Several dozen of these megachurches have expanded their role as they seek to be of assistance to other congregations. At least twenty are training students for the parish ministry. Others provide an intensive year-long intern experience for seminary students. At least five dozen American large-program churches own and operate attractive retreat centers that are available for use by outside groups. Most of these are higher quality facilities than the retreat centers built by parachurch groups in the 1960s or the denominationally owned camps. (The phenomenon of megachurches servicing people from other congregations may have advanced further in Korea than in the United States. The Kwang Lim Methodist Church in Seoul, for example, recently completed construction of a prayer center an hour south of the city that can seat 3,500 in the auditorium, includes sleeping accommodations for 600, and frequently is utilized by people from other congregations.)

An increasing number of large-program churches encourage staff members to serve occasionally as outside third-party parish consultants to other churches. Other staff members accept invitations to come in to help another congregation initiate a new specialized ministry or to direct a capital funds campaign or to deliver a series of lectures or to teach an adult class.

From a long-term perspective, perhaps the most significant dimension of this is the growing number of large-program churches that have installed facilities that equal the quality network television, including highly skilled technical staff to produce videotapes. The denominational leader in this is the United Church of Christ, thanks to the initiative of the Board of Homeland Ministries. (In 1991 the combined viewership of twenty UCC congregations with a television ministry exceeded the combined worship attendance of the nearly 6,400 congregations in that denomination.) In the years ahead more program churches will have the uplink to a satellite, and a growing number of congregations will have the capability of receiving signals directly from satellites. This will enhance the opportunities for these program churches to service other congregations with both inspirational and educational resources. It is still too early to discern whether theological seminaries will try to compete in that market.

The increasing popularity of videotapes as teaching tools raises an interesting issue. Who will be the major supplier of adult Bible study resources in the video era of 1999? Denominational headquarters? Parachurch organizations? Independent evangelists? Theological seminaries? Councils of churches? From today's perspective the leading candidate appears to be the large seven-day-a-week program churches that are on the cutting edge of innovative programming.

The Teaching Church

One reason for that prediction is the growing number of very large congregations that are accepting the role of serving as teaching churches. They are the contemporary successors of the old practice of inviting the senior minister of a large and growing church to "come to our church and share with our people what you've been doing and how you did it."

Among the most common products of that approach were these five: (1) It inflated the ego of the visiting speaker. (2) It proved to the people back in the speaker's home congregation that "we're a nationally famous success story, and others are eager to copy what we're doing." (3) It provided a supplemental income stream for the speaker. (4) It helped to sell books written by that speaker. (5) The story told by that speaker usually was so powerful and so impressive it often aroused one of three reactions among the listeners in the host church: (a) "My! Isn't that wonderful! I would like to visit that church some day, but I don't think I would want to be a member of a church like that"; or (b) "Maybe if we had a better minister, we could do that"; or (c) "That sounds great, but we could never do that here with our limited resources."

If the goal is for changed people and a changed congregation, a far more productive approach is for five to ten leaders from the church seeking to improve its ministry to go and spend two to five days at the teaching church with leaders from that congregation.

One expression of this role is to schedule two or three workshops annually under the generic umbrella, "This is what we have accomplished, this is how we did it, this is what we have learned, and this is what we believe you can take home that is exportable from our experiences." The specifics range from staffing to church growth to ministries with formerly married adults to how to implement a plan for relocating the meeting place to stewardship to adult Christian education to community ministries to planting or "parenting" new missions to enlisting missionaries to operating a Christian day school to the rehabilitation of deteriorated housing to preaching clinics to how to create a new organization to evangelism to the use of a new curriculum for Bible study to how to break that 450-500 barrier in worship attendance to creating mutual support groups for the victims of substance abuse to new approaches to church music to planning economic development programs in low-income communities. The production and marketing of videotapes is completely compatible with the role of a teaching church.

Another force behind the emergence of more teaching churches can be traced back to the 1960s. That era brought an increasing number of complaints that theological seminaries were preparing students, not for the parish ministry, but to go on to graduate school, where they would be prepared to become seminary teachers. Several theological seminaries undertook a variety of efforts to relate seminary education more closely to the "real world" in general and to the parish ministry in particular. One outcome was the required year as an intern in a parish. Another was to utilize the assets of a parachurch organization or a regional judicatory for "practical" field work experiences. A third was to turn to parachurch organizations for post-seminary training of those graduates who chose to go into the pastoral ministry.

One current approach is to begin to attack the issue at the point of the recruitment and training of the next generation of pastors. Once upon a time the standard sequence for a church member who experienced the call to go into full-time Christian service was to leave that congregation and go off to seminary. That meant being socialized into and by the culture of the theological seminary.

Today a growing number of the very large program churches offer a different sequence. A typical sequence begins with the member who becomes an active volunteer in one of these large full-service churches. Eventually a few are invited to join the paid program staff on a part-time or full-time basis. Through on-the-job training they are prepared to serve as pastors, youth directors, ministers of music, program specialists, directors of early childhood development centers, church business administrators, executive pastors, evangelists, program directors, creators of television ministries, teachers, communications experts, and associate ministers. Some leave to join the staff of another full-service church. Others continue on the staff of the congregation they had joined earlier as a new member.

If their sense of call includes the need for ordination, they usually choose one of two alternatives. Many continue on the staff while commuting to seminary for the required classroom and library work. Others never leave the campus of that seven-day-a-week church. The academic preparation required for ordination is fulfilled in the classrooms and library on that campus. These courses may be staffed by the faculty from an accredited theological seminary that has an extension center on that congregation's campus. Or the classes may be staffed by teachers from the membership of that large church, including the senior pastor.

In either case, the primary socializing experience that influences how that person does ministry is the parish setting, not an academic community. More significant, that candidate is socialized into how ministry is carried out in the large program church, not in a generic version of the worshiping community or in a small congregation.

It is reasonable to assume that theological seminaries will continue to prepare most of the ministers who go out to serve congregations averaging a hundred to three hundred at worship, but the teaching churches may become the number-one source of staff members and senior pastors for the very large program churches of American Protestantism.

Who Becomes a Teaching Church?

The number of teaching churches is growing at a remarkable pace. Every year brings an increase in the number of conferences designed to bring together leaders from self-identified teaching churches. This does not mean, however, that every large-program church should accept the additional responsibilities that go with being a teaching church. The best teaching churches display all seven of the following characteristics.

First, and by far the most important, the decision to accept this role came in response to what was perceived as a genuine call from God, not from ego needs or a desire for self-aggrandizement or a lust for fame. Ideally, acceptance requires sacrifice.

Second, the volunteer leaders understand that this is a servant role, not a new revenue source.

Third, the staff, both paid and volunteer, participate expecting to learn as well as to share.

Fourth, and perhaps most obvious, the teaching church must have something worthwhile to share with others out of the experiences of that teaching church.

Fifth, and this may be the most subtle, the best teaching churches display the capability of conceptualizing and acting out that role rather than focusing simply on workshops or "show and tell" or tours. When the participants leave, they should take with them a sense of the culture of the teaching church. The intangible and the subjective should not be concealed by an excessive emphasis on the mechanics of "how to do this."

Sixth, the leaders, instructors, and resource people should possess a high level of competence in transmitting abstract concepts, in responding to questions, and in challenging participants to adapt what they have seen, heard, and learned to their own situations "back home."

Seventh, the good teaching churches do not oversimplify. They recognize the power of local traditions, they affirm the differences among congregations, and they understand that simple answers to complex questions often are counterproductive.[13]

Will They Replace Denominations?

At this point in history the big unknown in describing the emerging role of the very large program churches is whether they will become the successor of what we have known as denominations.

For decades the responsibilities of American denominations have included recruiting and sending missionaries to other continents; enlisting, training, and ordaining persons with a call to the full-time Christian ministry; organizing or planting new churches; writing and publishing adult Bible study materials and training leaders to use those resources; organizing and operating Christian colleges, universities, and theological seminaries; providing financial assistance to other congregations in need; visiting those in prison; offering continuing education events to both the laity and the clergy; staffing campus ministries; publishing and selling hymnals, resources for worship, and books for a Christian audience; promoting interfaith dialogue; feeding the hungry; sheltering the homeless; building and operating orphanages, children's homes, retirement centers, and nursing homes; lobbying governmental agencies and legislative bodies; convening and managing huge inspirational events that attract participants from all over the globe; providing consultation services to congregations; owning and operating Christian elementary schools and Christian high schools; providing homes for unwed mothers; preaching the gospel to radio and television audiences; promoting peace and social justice; operating camps and retreat centers; offering conferences for attorneys, physicians, scientists, educators, governmental officials, and others who want to go away for a few days and reflect with a peer group on what the Gospel says to how they practice their vocation; management of a pension system for full-time workers in a Christian vocation; and loaning money to new congregations for building programs.

Although that is not offered as an exhaustive list, it is significant for one reason. Today one can pick any item on that list and find at least a few full-service program churches that are offering that service or that ministry.

What is the unique role left for denominational agencies? Accountability of the churches to one another? The redistribution of income? Setting and maintaining standards for ordination? Influencing public policy and foreign relations? Transmitting the orthodox faith from generation to generation and combating heresy? Providing for retired ministers in financial distress and for their needy survivors? Facilitating the merger of local churches? Training teachers for theological seminaries? Identifying emerging needs and creating new ministries in response to those needs and issues? Which of those can be carried out most effectively by denominations and which by the very large program churches?

In discussing what he describes as "the reconfiguration of American religion," James P. Wind has written, "Denominations used to be primary supporters of congregational identity . . . they now find themselves filling new fiscal, regulatory, and public policy roles."[14]

While this may distress many readers, the trends identified in this chapter suggest that the appeal of interchurch (and interdenominational) cooperation, institutional loyalties, the acceptance of closed denominational systems, ecumenism, and adherence to a denominational party line are being replaced by a demand for performance and quality and by greater competition among the churches for future generations of new members.

What's in a Name?

A few readers may insist that one of the unique contributions of denominations has been and continues to be providing a brand-name identity for congregations. It often is assumed that the denominational name conveys to people a particular theological or doctrinal or liturgical position. It is true that for many of us the distinctive identity is in the name. That generalization has applied to political parties, family trees, automobiles, cities, professional sports teams, state university systems, motels and hotels, shoes, restaurants, soaps, and hundreds of other consumer products. For generations it also has applied to American Protestantism. *Lutheran* or *Episcopal* or *Presbyterian* or *Southern Baptist* or *Methodist* or *Congregational* or *Reformed* or *Seventh Day Adventist* have conveyed a more precise identity than the simpler term *Christian*. Perhaps the one unique contribution of a denomination is the image conveyed by that name. Or has the changing face of American Christianity made that an obsolete concept?

The General Motors Corporation unveiled a completely new automobile in late 1990, called the Saturn. The Saturn name appeared in eight places on the new car, including the rear bumper, the steering wheel, the radiator shroud, the floor mats, both front quarter panels, and the hood. The GM name or logo could not be found on this new vehicle. And neither the General Motors name nor its logo is displayed on signs at dealerships. One official explained, ''Our target buyers are those who never set foot in a domestic store and wouldn't be caught dead in a GM dealership.''

General Motors paid the salaries of the people who designed the new car, of those who prepared the marketing campaign, and of the workers on the assembly line. It also financed the construction of a completely new plant in Spring Hill, Tennessee. The one thing General Motors did not do was to place its name on this new automobile.

A parallel appeared on the American church scene centuries ago. Many Anglican (now Episcopal) parishes carried names like Trinity Church or St. Paul's Church. Likewise the typical Roman Catholic parish rarely is marked by a sign that carries the name of that religious body. The Church of the Holy Family or Our Lady of Mercy or St. Elizabeth Seton Parish or St. Joan of Arc Church are deemed to be sufficient.

By contrast, most Protestant congregations have proudly flaunted the denominational label, often as the middle word. First Baptist Church, Westminster Presbyterian Church, Asbury Methodist Church, Concordia Lutheran Church, Peace Reformed Church, and Central Christian Church are among the more common examples.

In recent years, however, many congregational leaders have concluded that a denominational label may be more of a liability than an asset. It may be sending messages that are perceived as exclusionary or that carry a misleading image. Community of Joy, House of Hope, Calvary Temple, Wooddale Church, Vineyard Christian Fellowship, Capital City Christian Center, Faith Chapel, Gateway Cathedral, Willow Creek Community Church, Shepherd of the Valley, The Church of the Savior, The Chapel, New Life Fellowship, Christian Life Center, and Bible Fellowship are examples of this contemporary value system in choosing a name for a religious community.

A more recent change also is illustrated by twelve of these fifteen examples. That is the omission of the word *church* from the legal name. With some congregations this "just happened." The name chosen would make the word *church* appear to be redundant or superfluous. Another explanation is that the word *church* reinforces the Sunday morning image. "We have a seven-day-a-week ministry, so we picked a less confining name." The word *center* or the word *community* is more compatible than the word *church* with that seven-day-a-week role. The most common replacements include *community, center, cathedral, chapel, temple, house,* and *fellowship.*

The third change reflects the disappearance of the geographical parish. Several decades ago it was common practice to identify the general location of the meeting place in the name chosen for that congregation. Examples include Fourth Street Baptist Church, the East Side Church of God, North Methodist Church, University Presbyterian Church, and High Street Christian Church. Today the self-identified regional church avoids limiting its outreach by choosing a name that does not suggest a narrow geographical service area.

All three of these changes are consistent with the goal of conveying a clear image. That is the image of an open, inclusive, active, live, vital, vibrant, and joyous community of Christians. The first-time visitor should not feel excluded because of denominational heritage, place of residence, or other irrelevant stereotypes.

The fourth, the most subtle, and perhaps the least significant change also is consistent with the goal of conveying a clear and memorable image. Researchers have found that the easiest names to remember consist of three or five syllables. Thus names such as Calvary Temple, Faith Chapel, and Gateway Cathedral meet all four of these criteria. They do not suggest an exclusionary denominational identity, they do not include the word *church,* they do not reflect a neighborhood orientation, and they have three to five syllables.

What's in a name? Maybe not much, but the names chosen by many of the new and very large program churches are consistent with what many label "the postdenominational era."

The thesis of this book is that one of the most influential and far-reaching developments in the changing face of American Protestantism has been the decline of the Sunday morning church and the emergence of hundreds of large and rapidly growing full-service program churches that offer a seven-day-a-week ministry. That change is so great it deserves a separate chapter.

CHAPTER TWO

From Sunday Morning to Seven Days a Week

When I arrived nine years ago, several of the old-timers were still looking back wistfully to when this was the most prestigious church serving the most prestigious people living in the most prestigious neighborhood in the city," recalled the forty-seven-year-old senior minister of what is now a seven-day-a-week congregation that averages well over eight hundred at Sunday morning worship.

"This congregation had been organized in 1948, and the first unit was completed three years later on a half-acre site across the street from a brand-new elementary school. At the time this was on the far west side of the city, but it soon was fully developed with expensive single-family homes on quarter-acre lots," continued this visionary pastor. "Worship attendance peaked at well over five hundred in about 1960, a couple of years before the founding pastor retired. He was followed by a young firebrand who saw his role as being the prophetic voice of Christianity, and attendance plummeted. When he left in 1967, the Sunday school was averaging less than a hundred and worship attendance was down to a little under two hundred. After that experience, the pendulum swung, and the third minister was a man who believed it was possible to re-create the 1950s—and that's what the people wanted. He was an excellent preacher, and he went out and found an inspiring minister of music, who organized what people here claimed was one of the best chancel choirs in the nation, plus an adult handbell choir, a brass quartet, and a couple of other choirs for children and youth."

"You're telling me he was successful in re-creating yesterday?" asked the visitor incredulously.

"Almost," replied the current pastor. "Church attendance more than doubled and peaked at nearly five hundred in 1973. They spent over a million dollars renovating the buildings that were now over twenty years old. They also acquired two adjacent lots and razed the houses for off-street parking. The air began to go out of the balloon when the elementary school across the street closed and the building was turned into a senior citizens' center. That symbolized what had been happening here for several years. What had been a neighborhood of young families in the 1950s had changed. Most of the houses were now occupied by widows and retired couples, many of whom spent two or three months every winter in the Sunbelt. Most of the younger families moving in were Roman Catholic. That remarkable choir director was divorced in 1974 and left a couple of months later. While this church has always had a strong adult Sunday school, the children's division began to run out of kids. When the Director of Christian Education retired in 1975, the decision was made to replace that position with an older minister who was responsible for the pastoral care of the people and visiting the growing number of shut-ins."

"What happened next?" came the question.

"To make a long story short, that minister left in 1977 after a ten year pastorate. The successor is one of the most sincere and genuine Christians I have ever met, but according to the people here, he was at best an average preacher. He excelled in one-to-one relationships and apparently made the pastoral care of people his number-one priority. As the members continued to grow older, replacements weren't found for those who died or moved away, and the attendance dropped. That inflationary wave of the 1970s forced the congregation to cut back on staff. That reinforced the pattern of numerical decline."

"Sounds to me as if what had been a classic illustration of the Sunday morning church of the 1950s built around great preaching, great music, the adult Sunday school, and excellent pastoral care of the members gradually evolved into a congregation organized around a network of friendship ties, past shared experiences, and one-to-one relationships with your predecessor at the hub of those one-to-one relationships," observed the visitor.[1]

"Exactly," replied the current pastor. "The one exception I would make to your description is that they were able to make that Sunday morning model work into the mid-1970s.''

"I won't quarrel with that," replied the visitor, "but apparently the reason it still worked was that the focus continued to be on people born during the first four decades of this century. It's hard to build a Sunday morning church today that will attract large numbers of people born since 1955.''

"That became my basic premise shortly after I arrived," replied the pastor. "It took me about six weeks to come to that same conclusion. I was faced with an aging membership that was down to an average attendance of about two hundred at worship. The death rate of our membership for the previous four years averaged out to 3.3 per 100 members annually, triple that of the American population age 14 and over. We were meeting in an aging and obsolete set of buildings on a one-acre parcel of land that had sixty off-street parking spaces. Houses in this neighborhood were selling at the time for $100,000 to $125,000. That translated into $400,000 to $500,000 an acre for expanding this site.''

"That's expensive land. What did you do?" came the next question.

"After I had been here about three months, I invited to our home seven of the most influential and widely respected members," came the reply. "I explained to them that I was thirty-eight years old and I hoped this would be my last pastorate. Five of the seven were past sixty at the time. I asked them if I could count on their support for the next twenty-five years. One widow raised her hand. One man replied he wished he could promise that support, but he didn't think he would be around for another twenty-five years. The youngest leader in that group surprised everyone, including me, by announcing that she would be leaving the following month to accept a promotion in her company that would take her to Seattle. After we adjusted to that shock, everyone soon agreed that the future volunteer leadership would not be coming from the people in that room.''

"I'm a little surprised they were so agreeable," commented the visitor. "As a general rule, people resent it when confronted with the fact that the end of an era has arrived.''

"I didn't say that to them, although that was my basic premise," corrected the pastor. "I let them tell one another that the end of an era had arrived. Actually, of course, the end of that Sunday morning church era

39

had come back when my predecessor's predecessor had left. It also helped that I was by far the youngest person in the room, so it was apparent that even though I was a newcomer, I had the greatest investment in the future.''

''Did you drop any more bombs that evening?'' questioned the visitor.

''No, my basic rule is only one bomb per meeting, so I asked them if we could meet again in two weeks to talk some more,'' recalled the pastor. ''I am convinced that most of us normal people do our best thinking on the way home from meetings. So, before they left, I repeated two points. The first was the one I had made: I expected to be here for another twenty-five to thirty years. The second was the one they made: If I planned to stay that long, we would have to recruit a new generation of leaders in the years ahead.''

''What did you do at that next meeting?'' asked the visitor.

''We spent about an hour reflecting on that first meeting and gave everyone a chance to share second thoughts,'' recalled this patient and persuasive pastor. ''Several wanted me to tell them what we should do next. With great difficulty I resisted that invitation. Eventually the one charter member in that group suggested that maybe we should create a futures committee. As soon as he finished making that suggestion, I affirmed it as strongly as I could, and another person offered to introduce it at our next board meeting. She did, the board agreed, a futures committee was selected and began to meet.[2] By the end of the fourth meeting of that group, every person except one agreed that our future was severely limited in those obsolete buildings on that inadequate site at that well concealed location and that we should relocate to a larger and more accessible site with greater visibility and redefine our role as a seven-day-a-week regional church.''

''This came as a complete surprise to you?'' inquired the visitor solemnly.

''Not exactly,'' smiled the pastor with a grin that reminded the visitor of the cat who had eaten the canary. ''But it was easier and faster than I had expected. One reason we had less difficulty and opposition than we might have encountered was that two of the seven people I had met with earlier in those informal meetings were on this futures committee. A second reason was that I replaced them on that original ad hoc group with five other old-timers, and we met in our home once every month or so to talk about the deliberations of that futures committee.''

"Another reason was that you were an active leader in that futures committee, weren't you?" challenged the visitor.

"I certainly was!" exclaimed the pastor. "I already told you I planned to stay for another twenty years. You don't think I would sit silently while someone else shaped my future!"

"Summarize for me the next eight years," requested the visitor. "I have to leave in five minutes."

"That futures committee recommended that we relocate, and we spent six months trying to find the right parcel of land. Providentially, just as we were beginning to despair of ever finding anything that would be suitable, this eleven-acre site came on the market for $1.1 million. We sold the old property to a Greek Orthodox Church for $700,000. The unspoken bonus was that none of our members decided to stay with that sacred place and join the congregation that bought it. We have completed our first two building programs, and we start the third next year. We're a seven-day-a-week church that averages well over eight hundred at worship, and two-thirds of our new members were born after 1955."

"Any regrets?" asked the about-to-depart visitor.

"Yes, one big one," came the instant response. "For another two million dollars we could have bought the twelve acres immediately to the south. We chickened out because we were afraid of too much debt. Now it's covered with apartments, and our growth is limited. We just adopted a four-period Sunday morning schedule that runs from seven o'clock to noon in order to expand our teaching ministry. Over half of the total enrollment in our teaching ministry is scattered through the week, but we still average nearly eight hundred in Sunday school. If I had it to do over again, I would have insisted we buy both parcels."

The Road to Yesterday

"When I arrived here two years ago, I found a church that was badly overstaffed and trying to do more than the resources permitted," declared the fifty-six-year-old senior pastor at First Church. "They had staff trying to build programs that could be done better by social welfare agencies or by the government. Within eighteen months we cut the payroll by more than $100,000. For seven years they had been dipping into the endowment fund to cover the deficit in the operating budget. We eliminated one associate minister, two part-time people in music, one full-time secretary, a part-time receptionist, a full-time person in children's ministries, and one custodian. Many of the programs that this church was trying to do, but not very effectively, we turned over to secular agencies. Some of them are housed here, but they pay rent for their use of the building. For example, they were trying to run a child-care center here, and it was costing the church $30,000 a year beyond the income it generated. We turned that over to a woman who wanted to run her own program. She has only about half as many kids in it as the church's program, but it pays its way, and she gives the church $500 a month in lieu of rent. The adult day-care center has been turned over to an ecumenical group, and they operate it in a building owned by the city.''

"Don't your people object to this cutback in programming?'' inquired the visitor.

"No, they're delighted to see the budget in the black,'' declared the pastor. "In my first year we cut the deficit to less than $5,000. Last year we had a surplus, even though our receipts were down by $100,000. We've traded quantity for quality, and our people like that. We've cut back from seven choirs to two, but they're both top quality choirs. The sanctuary was two-thirds empty for the first service when I came, so we cut out that first service, and now we fill the sanctuary over half the Sundays in the year. People like it when the church is full.''

"What's happened to your attendance since you changed the schedule?'' asked the visitor.

"Naturally it's down a little,'' came the reply. "That's a predictable tradeoff. I knew that when we cut back to only one service we would show a modest drop in total attendance, but it was worth the price. We have a stronger sense of community, we're more unified, and we have a more efficient operation. We recognize that our people want a meaningful worship service with good music, an excellent Sunday school for their children, and a reasonable level of pastoral care. We're concentrating on the basics and saving money while we do it. People appreciate that.''

In two years the average attendance in this congregation dropped from 635 to 520. During the next five years it dropped to 370. At the end of seven years, this minister left the pastorate to accept a position as a fund raiser for a children's home. He was offered this position as a result of his reputation as an astute financial manager.

Many of the longtime members were sorry to see him leave. They appreciated his success in minimizing expenditures, and they preferred one worship service to two. Most favored this simpler schedule compared to the more complex arrangement they felt had produced ''two congregations'' and increased the level of anonymity. They felt more comfortable with the decrease in complexity, the enhanced intimacy, and the surplus at the end of every fiscal year, rather than a deficit. Some also voiced their greater comfort with the slower pace of congregational life during this new era.

These two examples illustrate one of the most far-reaching changes that has occurred within American Protestantism during the second half of the twentieth century. The Sunday morning church has been succeeded by the seven-day-a-week parish. To be more specific, the number of Protestant churchgoers who are satisfied with the Sunday morning church has been decreasing. Concurrently the number of people seeking the quality of ministry and the range of choices offered by the full-service program church with a seven-day-a-week schedule has been increasing at a remarkably rapid pace.

The combination of the emergence of the seven-day-a-week parish, the diminishing attraction of the Sunday morning church, and the preferences of churchgoers born after 1955 has presented most denominations and thousands of churches with a challenging fork in the road. The more comfortable of these two alternatives was chosen by the people in the second of these two brief case studies. This is to continue as a Sunday morning church while growing older and smaller. This choice usually produces fewer stresses, conflicts, and challenges. It is less demanding and cheaper. It does not threaten tradition, long-established relationships, or the status quo. It enhances intimacy rather than increasing the level of anonymity. It is an extremely popular path to follow.

The alternative, which was illustrated by the opening case study, is far more difficult, stress producing, expensive, and challenging. This path is filled with change. It is the decision to grow younger and larger by becoming a full-service church.

Almost all of the large and attractive Sunday morning churches that flourished during the middle third of this century have chosen one of these two forks in the road. The vast majority have taken the more comfortable path of growing older and smaller. Sometimes this process was facilitated by the premature departure of a highly effective minister and/or by a serious mismatch between the new pastor and that parish and/or by a counterproductive approach to planned change, which caused the people to reject that vision of what a new tomorrow could be, and/or by substituting denominational goals for a congregational vision and/or the vote of the people for the illusion of continuity over the fear of discontinuity.[3]

The only compatible and supportive environments left for the Sunday morning churches are in retirement communities that include large numbers of mature adults, the winter visitor churches in the Sunbelt, and the communities that attract tourists from all over the continent.

In a few other places, one or two large churches have accepted the challenge to perpetuate yesterday and have succeeded thanks to the combination of a superb preacher, an exceptionally competent minister of music, a loving and remarkably productive minister of pastoral care, and a highly skilled staff specialist who built and maintained that network of adult Sunday school classes.

A somewhat larger number have successfully made the transition from 1955 to 1995 by evolving into seven-day-a-week churches. For many this transformation was facilitated by the relocation of the meeting place and the construction of new facilities clearly designed to house a seven-day-a-week ministry. For others, the primary factor in this transformation was the arrival of a new senior minister.

The largest number of the full-service churches of today, however, have been organized since 1960 and thus never had to battle that long-established tradition of concentrating most of the resources on Sunday morning.

One generous estimate is that the number of these large member-oriented program churches designed to respond to the needs and concerns of the generations born after World War II doubled between 1978 and 1988, and that number now exceeds 10,000.[4]

This is part of a larger long-term trend that has brought a tripling in the size of the average church during the twentieth century. In 1990 Roman Catholic parishes in the United States averaged 2,380 baptized souls per congregation, compared to 1,290 in 1906 and 860 in 1890. *The Census of Religious Bodies of 1890,* conducted by the United States Bureau of the Census, reported 153,054 Protestant congregations with a combined total of 14 million members, or an average of 91 members per church.

One source reported a total of 350,481 congregations with 145.4 million members in 1990.[5] If the Roman Catholic totals are deducted from those figures, that leaves 327,300 congregations with 90 million members, or an average of 275 members per church.

During the course of the twentieth century, the Southern Baptist Convention is expected to nearly double the number of congregations from 19,558 in 1900 to nearly 40,000 in 2000, but the baptized membership probably will increase tenfold. The average number of members per congregation rose from 85 in 1900 to 395 in 1989.

The six predecessor denominations of what is now The United Methodist Church reported a combined total of slightly over 56,000 congregations in 1906 with 5.3 million members—an average of 95 members per church. By 1990 the number of congregations had dropped to 37,500, but the total membership had climbed to 8.8 million, or an average of 235 members per church, down from an average of 265 in 1969.

Protestant churches, like other institutions in American society, are continuing to evolve, and many are getting larger and larger. To focus only on size, however, greatly oversimplifies a complex subject, since many of the most significant changes are in purpose, role, style, and priorities. The medical clinic is replacing the general practitioner who worked alone. Corporate agriculture is replacing the small family farm. The large supermarket is taking most of the business from the "Mom & Pop" grocery. The shopping mall has replaced Main Street as the center of retail trade.

Perhaps the most useful analogy for examining how the large full-service church with a seven-day-a-week program is the successor to the Sunday morning church of the 1950s is to review what has happened to private four-year liberal arts colleges, which also flourished in the 1950s and into the 1970s.

From Liberal Arts College to Professional School

While doing research on a book on the future of private liberal arts colleges, David W. Breneman made a startling discovery. This former president of Kalamazoo College assumed that approximately 600 of the 2,100 four-year colleges and universities in the United States fit into this category. Back in 1970 the Carnegie Foundation had counted a total of 689 private liberal arts colleges. Twenty years later Breneman counted

212 schools that met his definition. Several had closed, but most of that drop in numbers could be traced to two changes. Eleven of the group had evolved into small universities, offering a range of graduate degrees. The big change, however, was that most of the others had become primarily small professional colleges. Fewer than 40 percent of the graduates received a liberal arts degree. The majority of degrees were in professional fields such as business, engineering, education, nursing, computer science, and agriculture.[6]

Breneman concludes that pressures of the marketplace are forcing many of the small liberal arts colleges to redefine their role and to become more concerned with preparing students for the labor force. It also should be noted that scores of these small schools that once operated on a five-day-a-week schedule now offer evening and weekend classes.

Another perspective for examining the same issue is to note the change in enrollment patterns. As recently as 1950 private colleges and universities accounted for nearly one-half of the total enrollment in all institutions of higher education in the United States. By 1960 that proportion had dropped to only 43 percent. Thirty years later that proportion was only 22 percent—and that figure includes the enrollment at dozens of big private universities such as Harvard, Notre Dame, Emory, Stanford, Yale, Southern Methodist, Chicago, Vanderbilt, Northwestern, Boston, Duke, Georgetown, Johns Hopkins, Columbia, and Princeton as well as the smaller four-year private schools. The big state universities and the two-year community colleges accounted for most of that fivefold increase in enrollment during the past four decades.

There is still a place for the small, four-year, private, liberal arts college with its emphasis on education for the joy of learning, the sense of community, the fellowship between faculty and undergraduates, the affirmation and transmission of shared values, and the rewards for excellence in teaching. It must be recognized, however, that an increasingly large proportion of college-bound young people are picking a different alternative from that huge array of choices before every high school graduate.

The Ecclesiastical Parallel

A parallel pattern can be identified on the ecclesiastical scene. Up through the 1940s the majority of Protestant churchgoers in the United

States worshiped with small to middle-sized congregations. This is still true today in several denominational families.

A reasonable estimate is that approximately 80,000 Protestant churches in the United States report fewer than one hundred members. The four million members of these small churches suggest that a market demand still exists for the worshiping community that places a high value on friendliness, intimacy, kinship ties, local traditions, spontaneity, and informality.

A better yardstick, however, for measuring change is to count people, not institutions. As was pointed out earlier, the private liberal arts colleges and universities no longer are able to attract the same proportion of college-bound people as they once did. Their market share of the total enrollment dropped by more than one-half in the four decades following 1950.

Likewise the small churches are attracting a shrinking proportion of Protestant churchgoers in the United States. Like the big public universities, the very large churches are attracting an ever-growing share of the churchgoing market, especially the generations born after 1940. While it is true that 37 percent of all congregations affiliated with the Presbyterian Church (USA) report fewer than a hundred members, they account for 8 percent of the total membership of that denomination. At the other end of the size scale, the 424 congregations that reported more than a thousand members in 1988 represented only 3.5 percent of all churches, but included 23 percent of all members in that denomination. In this denomination one-half of all members can be found in 15 percent of the churches.

The United Methodist Church reports that 13 percent of the 37,500 congregations in that denomination include one-half of all members. On the average Sunday morning the smallest 10,800 congregations report a combined worship attendance of 235,000, the same as reported by the 350 largest churches.

Southern Baptists report that 14 percent of their churches include one-half of the members. In the Evangelical Lutheran Church in America, which has relatively few tiny congregations, 19 percent of the parishes include one-half of the confirmed members. In the Lutheran Church—Missouri Synod one-half of the members can be found in 18.5 percent of the congregations.

The private liberal arts colleges are losing out in the marketplace for students born after 1950 to the large public universities, the small professional schools, and the community colleges. Likewise the small churches are losing out in the quest for younger members to the large full-service program churches.

This analogy is useful from another perspective. Back in the middle of the twentieth century, the private liberal arts four-year college was widely accepted as the model for post-high school education. That model was an effective response to the demand of the market. It could be argued that the private liberal arts four-year college defined the market. It certainly represented the accepted model for the church-sponsored colleges of 1940 or 1950 designed to reach students born in the 1920–1940 era.

On the congregational scene the accepted model for American Protestantism was the Sunday morning parish that combined worship, preaching, Sunday school, intercessory prayer, fellowship, and pastoral care into one attractive package. As was pointed out earlier, a widely used formula for success at old First Church Downtown was "great preaching, great music, and a great Sunday school." Add to that formula the winsome personality of a gregarious pastor, the presence of a dozen prestigious community leaders, an impressive edifice, and a reasonable level of pastoral care, and success was practically guaranteed in attracting the generations born before 1940.

What Happened?

Two changes have forced both the private liberal arts four-year colleges and the churches to redefine their roles. The first was the arrival of new generations of potential customers. The second was that the expectations of the younger generations differed greatly from the expectations of previous generations.

The vast majority of both college students and church members born before 1940 appeared willing to conform to the culture and agenda of the institutions designed to serve them. For decade after decade each new generation was socialized into a culture that taught young people how to fit into existing patterns of behavior, to accept the traditional norms, and to adapt to the agendas of long-established institutions. The emergence of labor unions in the nineteenth century, the revolution in American agriculture that began in the 1930s, and the occasional election of a third-party candidate for public office were among the highly visible exceptions to this pattern of accommodating traditional norms.

The generations born after 1940 challenged this idea of conformity to inherited expectations, habits, and traditions. The campus unrest of the 1960s, the resistance to the conflict in Vietnam, the challenge to traditional dress codes, the rapid increase in the number of unmarried couples living together, the increase in the number of never-married mothers, the doubling of the proportion of adult women employed outside the home, the decision by the federal government to use inflation rather than deflation as a response to economic disruptions, the postponement of marriage and motherhood, and the separation of the place of residence from the place of employment stand out among the changes initiated by the generations born after 1940.

One of the most widely discussed results has been the emergence of what often is labeled "the consumer society." Automobile manufacturers are now expected to design cars that meet the needs of the buying public, rather than vehicles that will produce the biggest profit margins. When the armed forces of the United States replaced the draft with volunteers, that meant accepting a far greater proportion of mothers, fathers, and single parents. Factories are expected to be as concerned about the environment as they are with creating jobs or making money. Employers are expected to devise working conditions that accommodate the health and life-style of the employee, rather than demanding that all employees be willing to sacrifice their own personal needs in favor of a more efficient workplace.

Colleges and universities are now designing academic schedules and courses to meet the expectations of potential students rather than assuming that the students will flock to a set of courses and a schedule designed by that institution of higher education. For scores of educators the biggest shock came when it was realized that the community college is not a two-year transition between high school and the junior year in a senior college or university. For the vast majority of students enrolled in these institutions, the community college is the transition between school and the labor force, not advanced education.

The parallel in American Protestantism is the gradual shrinkage in the number of adults who are satisfied with the offerings of the Sunday morning church and a sharp increase in the number of those who are seeking a full-service church with a seven-day-a-week program.

"When did you first set foot on this property?" is a question I have asked thousands of adults who are recent new members of a particular congregation.

The vast majority of new members born before 1930 reply that their first visit was on a Sunday morning. A few refer to a funeral or wedding, and an even smaller number recall that their first visit was on Christmas Eve.

The majority of those born after 1950 look back to a weekday or a weeknight event as the occasion of their first visit. That list includes Mothers' Morning Out, a Tuesday evening Bible study group, Christmas Eve, bringing a child to the weekday early childhood development center or nursery school, a Wednesday evening film on family problems, an invitation to work as a volunteer in a food pantry program, a Thursday evening mutual support group, a Saturday afternoon softball game, the Monday evening meeting of a new circle in the women's organization, a Sunday evening worship service, a New Year's Eve prayer vigil, helping to pioneer a Tuesday morning Mothers' Club, a Saturday evening event for young single adults, a Friday evening party after the high school football game, a Thursday evening Inquirers' Class, volunteering to serve noon meals to the hungry, a Tuesday morning music encounter event for preschool children, a Monday night meeting of a substance abuse support group, a Saturday afternoon seminar for those involved in a traumatic divorce experience, a coed volleyball game for parents of young children, a Tuesday evening prayer and praise service, the Sing-Along Messiah, an eight-week series of parenting classes, a Saturday evening worship experience, the wedding of a friend or relative, an organ concert, the organization of a local chapter of Habitat for Humanity, volunteering to work one evening a month in a program to shelter the homeless, or attending an evening class designed to help individuals file their income tax forms.

In simple terms, the principal entry point for prospective future members in large churches has moved from Sunday morning to seven mornings, seven afternoons, and seven evenings every week.

A more sophisticated explanation parallels what happened in higher education. Once upon a time high school graduates came to the four-year liberal arts college and accepted the schedule and the course of study the school offered. The product was a liberal arts education for the graduate. During the past two or three decades the students have been looking for a school that will give them a ticket that can be turned in for a job in the labor force. As a result, the majority of the surviving private four-year liberal arts colleges have evolved into either professional schools or small universities, but the terminal community college has taken a big chunk of what once was their market.

In a similar manner these new generations of churchgoers have walked onto the ecclesiastical stage and looked for a church that will be responsive to their personal, religious, spiritual, and family needs. Their parents and grandparents accepted with few questions the schedule and the offerings of the Sunday morning church. They were strongly influenced by geographical proximity, denominational allegiance, language, nationality and racial heritage, inherited loyalties, and kinship ties.

Sunday morning church is less attractive to these younger churchgoers than it was to earlier generations. One result is that literally hundreds of what once were Sunday morning congregations have been transformed, usually following the arrival of a new pastor, into seven-day-a-week churches.

Perhaps more highly visible, and certainly more widely studied and discussed, has been the founding since 1950 of four or five thousand rapidly growing and now very large Protestant churches that were designed to identify and respond to the spiritual and personal needs of people engaged in a religious quest.[7]

In several respects these seven-day-a-week churches resemble the community college. One parallel, of course, is the widespread use of the word *community* in the name. Far more important, however, is the fact that the program and the schedule are designed for the needs and convenience of the participants rather than the preferences of those in charge. That weekly schedule offers an unprecedented range of choices, including many events, services, and programs offered during the evening as well as in the daytime and on the weekend.

Both the community college and the seven-day-a-week church rely on specialized staff, rather than generalists, some of whom are part-time and many of whom do not carry the standard academic credentials. In both, the focus is on the needs of the client. In both, a highly redundant advertising program is designed to attract first-time visitors. In both, it is assumed that inherited institutional loyalties will carry little weight in attracting a new clientele, but word-of-mouth endorsements will be influential. In both, off-street parking is a critical part of the design in reaching commuters. In both, the real estate is designed to make it easy for the first-time visitor to find the right door. Both are attracting a large share of the market once served by small institutions.

Both accept the fact that this may be a transitional stage in the life of their clientele. A few of the two-year community college students do move on to graduate with a bachelor's degree from a four-year college or a university. Many more, however, see this as entrance into the labor force, not into a degree program. Both offer a growing variety of events, programs, and groups designed to aid the personal journey through life of the individual.[8]

Likewise, the typical seven-day-a-week church bids farewell to 10 to 20 percent of its members annually. A few die, many move away, and others leave for a less demanding Sunday morning church. For many, however, the transition is from a life without an active and continuing involvement in the ministry of any worshiping community to a new stage in which "church" ranks with family and job as one of the key focal points of the weekly routine. For others, the seven-day-a-week church is the transition between Roman Catholicism and a new religious pilgrimage in the Protestant tradition. For both groups, the seven-day-a-week church is a place to meet and make new friends and to grow old together with these friends who share what has become a common religious perspective.

In the community college, unlike at least a few colleges and universities, the instructors prepare their courses in response to the vocational needs of the students, not as an outgrowth of the teacher's current research or publication schedule. Likewise, the preachers and teachers in the seven-day-a-week church prepare their sermons and design their classes in response to the religious, personal, spiritual, and family needs of the people, rather than in response to their own religious pilgrimage or past seminary classroom experience or their own contemporary interests. In both, this evoked considerable criticism from the traditionalists who denounce this "consumer orientation."

In both, another factor behind these criticisms may be dismay over a shrinking clientele for the traditional approaches to higher education or to religion.

The generations born since 1940 not only have brought their own agendas, but also their emancipation from traditional expectations and inherited loyalties has forced hundreds of private four-year liberal arts colleges to redefine their role and to focus on the needs and agenda of the students. In a similar manner, these younger generations have encouraged the emergence of scores of professional schools, of hundreds of large and rapidly growing community colleges, and of thousands of large and rapidly growing full-service churches with a seven-day-a-week program.

One of the similarities, and also one of the differences, between these four-year professional colleges and the full-service churches is size. Most of the colleges report an enrollment between 500 and 2,000. Most of these full-service churches also report an average attendance at worship of between 500 and 2,000. The big difference is the rapid growth in the number of full-service churches that report an average worship attendance over 2,000.

Another parallel is that while many of the four-year colleges are reporting substantial increases in enrollment, others are facing a declining enrollment.

Likewise some Protestant denominations are reporting an increase in the number of large churches, while others are reporting a decrease. In 1950 the Southern Baptists reported 1,019 congregations with 1,000 or more members. By 1972 that total had doubled to 2,189, and by 1990 it had increased to nearly 3,000.

By contrast, the two predecessor denominations of The United Methodist Church reported 1,814 congregations with 1,000 or more members in 1965. By 1970 that total had dropped to 1,771, and by 1990 it was down to approximately 1,300.

That raises another question: Why do some of these full-service churches grow so large?

CHAPTER THREE

Why So Large?

Three of the most common characteristics of today's high quality seven-day-a-week churches are (1) they are attracting a disproportionately large number of people born after 1955, (2) they are very large congregations, and (3) they continue to attract large numbers of new members.

While it is an oversimplification, the first characteristic can be explained in one sentence: These churches are offering a meaningful and high-quality response to the religious needs of the people born during the second half of the twentieth century. One analogy could be with the motion picture *The Field of Dreams*. If you build a high-quality ministry with a strong teaching dimension, the people will come. For outsiders that may be a mystery, but the people do come in a never-ending stream, especially in the evening and during the weekend.

Far more controversial is the question of why so many of these churches become so large. One small slice of the explanation lies in the audience. Most adult Americans born since 1955 grew up in a world consisting of large and complex institutions that are filled with anonymity. That long list includes consolidated public elementary schools, large medical clinics with a dozen or more physicians on staff, giant grocery stores, superhighways, unbelievably large amusement parks, multiscreen motion picture theaters, shopping malls, high schools with more than a thousand students, forty-story office buildings, universities with tens of thousands of students on one campus, national television networks, three-car garages, big hospitals, and complex airports. The world they have grown up in taught most of them how to cope with large-scale institutions, complexity, anonymity, vast distances, a fast pace, impersonal directions, and megachurches. That world also has taught them how to meet and make new friends in a variety of complex settings.

By contrast, most of the Protestant churchgoers of 1940 grew up in a world filled with slow travel; strong kinship ties; county fairs; small movie houses that showed only one or two films every week; public transportation; small elementary schools; grocery stores in which the owner could call every customer by name; regional radio stations; a slower pace of life; powerful inherited loyalties, including language, nationality, race, and denominational self-identification; neighborhood-oriented institutions; short journeys from home to work; high schools with fewer than two hundred students; and small churches.

To some extent, the size of the religious institutions naturally will parallel the size of the secular institutions in any culture because they are subject to similar pressures.

Three Mavericks

"We promise people two things if they come to our church on Sunday morning," observed the fifty-seven-year-old theologically liberal senior minister of a one hundred-year-old downtown church that has tripled its worship attendance in fifteen years. "We promise when they leave, they will feel better than when they came, and we promise we will never go past twelve o'clock."

"When we changed the Sunday morning schedule to three worship services, we also broadened the range of choices we offer people," explained a pastor who claims a broad slice in the middle of the theological spectrum and who founded what is now a fourteen-year-old suburban church that averages nearly a thousand at worship.

"The first service is always built around Holy Communion, and my associate minister and I take turns preaching at that hour. The downstairs service at ten-thirty is built around preaching and contemporary music, most of which has been composed since 1965. The instrumental accompaniment usually includes drums, a couple of guitars, a keyboard, and one or two other stringed instruments. About once a month they also have a brass group. Our youngest associate preaches at that service about forty-five Sundays a year, they have a few guest preachers, and I try to preach there on every fifth Sunday. They offer Holy Communion the first Sunday of every quarter. Except for eight or ten Sundays a year, I preach at the upstairs service in the sanctuary at that same hour. We have a beautiful pipe organ, and about once a month we use the piano to accompany a children's choir. Our chancel choir sings at that service fifty Sundays a year."

"People today are biblically illiterate!" declared the self-identified theologically conservative senior minister of a large and rapidly growing independent congregation in the Midwest. "They want to know more about the faith, and the reason we're growing is because we meet that need. Both of our worship services run for nearly ninety minutes every Sunday morning with an hour in between for Sunday school. We use an overhead projector to flash the words of the choruses on screens so people can see them. Folks sing better with their chin up rather than with their chin buried in their chest. We teach the Bible and preach the Bible. We have a lively service, and no one objects to an hour and a half because we really love the Lord."

All three of these ministers believe strongly that worship should be filled with hope, joy, love, humor, a sense of celebration, a sensitivity to the needs that people bring with them when they come to church, and memorable sermons. All three carefully design a fast-paced worship service. All three are hard working, future oriented, visionary, good-natured, highly productive, creative, energetic, and enthusiastic leaders who enjoy the pastoral ministry.

All three of these ministers have been criticized repeatedly for what is described as their "excessive consumer orientation." All three have been criticized repeatedly by those who are convinced that the corporate worship of God should be dull, slow-paced, boring, humorless, and conducted in a monotone. All three have been criticized repeatedly by those who contend that each one enjoys being at the center of a "personality cult." All three have been criticized repeatedly because the rapid growth of their congregations represents clear evidence that they are not faithful to the Gospel. All three have been criticized repeatedly because each one operates on the assumption that participation in corporate worship is viewed by many Protestants as voluntary rather than as an obligation. All three have been criticized repeatedly for the centrality they give to hope in their preaching and for their neglect of legalisms, the harsh judgment of God, damnation, and hell. All three have been criticized repeatedly for compromising traditional principles or standards on divorce, remarriage, baptism, admission of non-members to the table of the Lord's Supper, the role of women in the church, instrumental music, weekday programming, racial segregation, educational requirements for program staff, and lack of cooperation with other churches and/or denominational agencies and meetings.

All three illustrate a common, but not universal, characteristic of the large and rapidly growing full-service church. All three display several characteristics of the innovative entrepreneur.[1]

All three fit the definition of maverick leaders, rather than of organizational managers. All three are vulnerable to the charge that they have built "a cult of personality."[2] All three carry little inherited baggage, and they often ignore tradition as they focus on being responsive to the contemporary religious and personal needs of seekers on a spiritual pilgrimage. They recognize that denominational priorities cannot be a substitute for a congregational vision. One result is that they often are perceived as not being "good team players."

Why have so many churches become so large in recent years?

The number-one reason is not location or favorable demographics or seven-day-a-week programming or a particular theological stance. The number-one factor, as was pointed out in the introduction to this book, is transformational leadership by a visionary pastor who knows how to rally people in support of a cause. To be more specific, these transformational leaders are completely convinced that people's lives can be transformed by the power of the Gospel. That is the number-one distinctive characteristic of these senior ministers.

In addition, these transformational leaders (1) can conceptualize a vision of a new tomorrow, (2) can articulate that vision so persuasively that people rally in support of it, and (3) know how to turn that vision into reality. These last two characteristics explain why business people often refer to these transformational pastors as entrepreneurial leaders. That is an accurate, but incomplete, description.

Why Do Some Become Very Large Churches?

Senior pastors who display all four of these characteristics are relatively scarce. That is one reason why the number of Protestant congregations averaging more than eighteen hundred at worship is counted in the hundreds, not the thousands. The market demand for very, very large churches exceeds the number of transformational pastors who display all four of those characteristics.

Most, but not all, of the very, very large Protestant congregations in the United States display a related characteristic that sets them apart from other churches. This characteristic can be described as two sides of a coin. Both are a product of that senior minister's conviction that the life of an individual can be transformed by the power of the Gospel. These very, very large congregations are filled with grateful people who testify eagerly and clearly that their lives have been transformed by what happened to them in and through that particular worshiping community. They identify themselves as transformed people.

This is not a new phenomenon. Paul talked and wrote about it repeatedly more than nineteen hundred years ago. John Wesley preached on it. It was a common phenomenon on the American frontier in the nineteenth century. The power of Jesus Christ has transformed the lives of people and of institutions for centuries.

The life of Paul offers a superb analogy for this phenomenon. The leaders who are most effective in proclaiming the transformational power of the Gospel are those who have experienced it personally. Those who can share their "before and after" experiences are more effective in telling the story than are most "birthright" Christians who have been reared in the faith. This may be the key in explaining the second half of what earlier was described as two sides of a coin.

Before moving on to that, however, a correction needs to be offered to conventional wisdom. A widely shared stereotype is that all the senior pastors of today's very large and rapidly growing full-service churches can be located somewhere on the most conservative one-fourth of the theological spectrum. That characterization applies to some, but far from all.

A better statement would be that most are theologically more conservative than the people they are seeking to reach. Thus many of today's senior ministers who fit in the broad middle of that theological spectrum have been remarkably effective in reaching large numbers of disillusioned former liberals, younger adults who were reared in a world that argued, "Parents should not try to impose their religious convictions on their children; the children should be encouraged to make their own decisions about their faith,'' and adults who grew up in a home without any church affiliation.

Perhaps an even more accurate description of contemporary reality, and one that alarms many theologians, seminary professors, and denominational leaders, is that the place that senior ministers occupy on the theological spectrum is relatively unimportant. The one exception is that the preacher must be a trinitarian. Three other variables are more significant than theological stance. One is that the senior minister holds a carefully worked out belief system that is internally consistent and coherent. (Incidentally, a Christ-centered belief system among these senior ministers is far more common than one in which God the Creator is the central figure of the Trinity.[3]) The second variable is the ability to communicate that belief system clearly and persuasively and to use it to shed light on the issues, questions, doubts, concerns, and problems the listeners bring with them to church. Relevance is in the mind of the listener, not in the manuscript of the preacher.

The third variable is that most of these preachers know their audience. Why do hundreds and hundreds of people come to church week after week? Many come longing to hear a word of hope that will transform their lives. They come praying for a word of comfort that will help them survive the coming week. They come wishing for a message that convinces them they are loved. When they have been loved and comforted and have had their faith restored, they are eager to return. The primary vehicle for transmitting that message is, of course, the messenger, not the sermon.

This leads into the second facet of this number-one reason for the growth of these large, full-service churches. When the sick have been healed, they want not only to share their joy, but also to encourage others to visit the place where they were healed. When the seekers have had their questions answered, they encourage others to experience what has changed their lives. Those who discover that their lives have been transformed by the power of Christ's love cannot avoid inviting others to come and share in that same experience. When the doubters have had their disbelief transformed into belief, they naturally seek to convert others to the truth. When those on a religious pilgrimage finally discover a church home that meets their needs, they often invite other pilgrims to join them.

While this generalization obviously does not apply to every member of these churches, it does explain why so many of the people in these large and rapidly growing churches do invite their friends, parents, colleagues at work, neighbors, and others to come to church with them. They persuasively invite others to come and share in that experience. The enthusiastic evangelistic efforts of these transformed individuals represent one of the biggest differences between the congregation that averages three hundred at worship and the one five times that size.

This, far more than demographic factors, explains why numerically growing congregations continue to grow and numerically shrinking churches continue to shrink. The great scientist Sir Isaac Newton explained a parallel phenomenon more than three centuries ago when he announced the first law of motion. Bodies in motion tend to remain in motion, and bodies at rest tend to remain at rest unless acted upon by some outside force.

In summary, the typical very, very large Protestant congregation often is led by a senior minister who has personally experienced the transformational power of Christ. This leads to the creation of a congregation of people who recognize their own lives have been transformed by the power of the Gospel. They in turn cannot help inviting others to come and be transformed.

This is the classic story of the persuasive enthusiasm of the new convert. In today's world of big institutions, this is one road to building the megachurch. It is not the only route, but it is the most heavily traveled road. This also helps to explain why so many of today's megachurches are still served by the founding pastor.

Is Worship Theater?

Back in the summer of 1988 George Plagenz, a widely syndicated religion writer, wrote a provocative column in which he compared the pulpit with the theater. He wrote: "Theater is something done with an audience in view. It must therefore be stimulating to the ear, the eye and the mind of the members of the audience. If preaching is theater, good preaching is good theater."[4] Plagenz devoted most of this brief essay to the importance of hope in preaching.

High on the list of reasons to explain the attractiveness and numerical growth of today's large seven-day-a-week churches is the combination of (1) a recognition of the centrality of the corporate worship of God in designing that weekly schedule, (2) an affirmation of the importance of hope in every sermon, and (3) an acting out of the importance of reaching the eye, the ear, the mind, the emotions, and the inner being of every worshiper. While they rarely use that analogy, these churches recognize that good worship must be good theater.

Good theater usually includes passion, humor, feeling, and a message that speaks to the human condition. The theatergoer leaves after a couple of hours, but that drama may stick in the mind and the soul for months and years to come. Likewise the effective proclamation of a transformational gospel requires an appeal to all the senses, not just the mind. In that same article, seminary-trained religion writer George Plagenz wrote: "It is the passionless quality of most preaching in the mainline (non-evangelical) churches that is keeping people away today." Almost by definition the proclamation of the transformational power of the Gospel will be filled with passion as well as with hope.

The proclamation of the transformational gospel is enhanced when it is done within the larger context of a worship experience that also is good theater. That entire worship experience often is built around the central theme of hope, and hope provides the thread of continuity. Hope is reinforced through prayers of intercession, various expressions of joy, love, and compassion, inspiring music, enthusiastic congregational singing, the reading of God's word, drama, affirmation, humor, celebration, visual imagery, illustrations, and the proclamation of the transforming gospel.

The more effectively this concept is implemented, the greater the intensity and volume of the criticisms from those who believe corporate worship should never be compared with drama or the theater, from those who are convinced worship should focus only on the confession of sin and prayer for forgiveness, from those who condemn laughter during worship, from those who know that corporate worship is a painful obligation a demanding God has imposed on sinful human beings, and from those who can accept a display of passion in politics or sports, but not in church.

The Evolution of the Liberal Agenda

Perhaps the most controversial explanation of why some congregations have become very large while others shrink is a product of the changing definition of a liberal theological position. For more than a decade following World War II, the thinking of the great German theologians dominated the teaching of theology in most of the American seminaries that influenced the mainline denominations. As Professor Sallie McFague has pointed out in a provocative essay, the agenda of that era was dominated by discussions of faith, history, reason, and revelation. She suggests that a critical issue of that era was "How can we *know* God?"[5]

An intellectual approach to the faith spoke to the religious needs of many in that era. Those years also brought into the mainline Protestant churches large numbers of people born after World War I, many of whom were socially, economically, politically, and especially theologically more liberal than their parents. For many liberals, a synonym for theological conservatives was "fundamentalists."

The early 1960s brought a change in the agenda for liberal American Protestantism. Questions directed at one's faith, at knowing God, and on the place of Jesus in religion gradually were replaced by a new social gospel that emphasized intervention into urban life, public policy, race relations, the redistribution of income, and the role of government. The focus on an intellectual approach to the faith was replaced by the call to action. This new goal of changing the world was reinforced in the late 1960s as liberation theology moved on to the theological agendas of liberal Protestants.

More recently, as Professor McFague points out, the newest shift has been to link together the fate of the oppressed and the fate of the planet. Social justice, peace, ecology, and the environment now dominate the agenda of liberal American Protestantism. The agenda has shifted from nurturing those on a faith journey to changing the world to saving the planet.

This paradigm shift in liberal theology did not occur in a vacuum. Several other changes were taking place concurrently. One was the emergence of evangelicalism as a force that was consistent with an expansion and fragmentation of the right two-thirds of the theological spectrum.[6] Theological moderates, evangelicals, and two or three groups of the self-identified "conservatives" moved onto the stage that had been occupied by the liberals of the 1950s. The liberal theological agenda of the 1950s became the agenda of the moderates and evangelicals in the 1990s. An interesting illustration is the twelve-volume commentary *The*

Interpreter's Bible, published by Abingdon Press in the 1950s. At that time it was perceived as a liberal commentary. Today it is accepted and widely used by self-identified conservative and evangelical pastors.

A second change that has had a tremendous impact on the mainline Protestant churches reflects the changing agendas of the theological seminaries. Back in the 1950s students often categorized professors by their theological positions. Professors were identified by such terms as *theologically liberal* or *conservative* or *neo-orthodox* or *middle-of-the-road.* In recent decades that continuum has been redefined with "theological" at one end and "ideological" at the other. Faculty members are identified by where they fall on that spectrum.

One product of that change in the agendas of seminaries is that many of the future pastors have a new perspective for deciding where they will go to school. They perceive many of the long-established seminaries related to the mainline Protestant denominations as being graduate schools of ideology that rally students in support of a cause being promoted by a few of the more highly visible faculty members. Many of the students born after 1955 declare that they prefer a professional school of theology designed to prepare people for the parish ministry.

As a result, many of the graduates of the graduate school of ideology do not enter the parish ministry. An increasing number leave the parish ministry after one or two pastorates. Others go from seminary to the parish with an ideological agenda in hopes of rallying the parishioners behind the latest cause. The young adults who were reared in a congregation affiliated with one of the mainline religious traditions, and who chose what they perceive to be a professional school preparing people for the parish ministry, subsequently discover their options are limited. They often are greeted with something between rejection and an unenthusiastic stance when they seek a pastorate in the denomination in which they were reared. They may be invited to join the staff of a large nondenominational full-service church as a program specialist. Or they may respond to a call to plant a new church for the denomination related to the seminary they attended. Or they may accept the call from a church affiliated with a theologically conservative religious tradition. Most do not return to the denomination in which they were reared.

Another change that coincided with the redefinition of the liberal theological agenda and with the shift in emphasis in scores of seminaries was the emergence of the Charismatic Renewal Movement in the late

1960s and the gradual maturing of this expression of the faith. With the exception of the hundreds of thousands of liberal Protestants who became part of the Charismatic Renewal Movement, this was largely written off as irrelevant or heretical by most liberals as well as by many fundamentalists.

One of the most significant changes turned out to be the biggest surprise of all to many parents born in the first third of this century, to officials and pastors in the mainline denominations, and to professors in most of the liberal seminaries. This was the appearance of that huge generation of churchgoers born in the 1956–68 era who, as a group, have turned out to be theologically more conservative than their parents.

A fifth development of the 1965–90 era was a product of several factors. One was the numerical shrinkage and the aging of the membership of tens of thousands of smaller and long-established congregations affiliated with the mainline Protestant denominations. A second was the high visibility acquired by the church growth movement during the 1970s and 1980s. A third resulted from the fact that the polity of most of these denominations overrepresented the voting power of smaller congregations and underrepresented the members of large churches at denominational conventions and conferences. A fourth was the change in the image held by many people of the large denominationally related church. Back in the 1950s they were viewed with respect, awe, and envy. Thirty years later they often were criticized for their selfish accumulation of an unfair share of scarce resources and for their unwillingness to give money, members, and other resources to small struggling congregations. Faithfulness to the gospel and numerical growth often were identified as incompatible goals. A fifth was that the increasing cost of health insurance, pensions, and other fringe benefits for pastors meant their total compensation was increasing at a faster pace than the rise in the Consumer Price Index.

Out of these and other motivating factors came the decision to devote large quantities of denominational resources to the "empowerment" and assistance of that increasing number of small congregations that were struggling to continue with a full-time resident pastor in an increasingly competitive ecclesiastical marketplace.

This deep concern with the institutional survival of these small aging congregations had only limited appeal to the generations born after World War II. It also caused many of the senior pastors, staff, and volunteer leaders in the large churches to feel ignored, neglected, and exploited. They were being asked to send more money to denominational headquarters, but not receiving the help they felt they needed to compete with that growing number of full-service program churches. Their anxiety grew as they looked around and saw so many of the big Sunday morning churches of the 1950s shrinking dramatically in size.

This shrinkage in the number of big mainline Protestant Sunday morning churches was especially visible in California, the Great Plains, the Northeast, and the Midwest. In 1988, for example, the number of United Methodist congregations reporting a thousand or more members in Iowa, Illinois, Indiana, Michigan, Ohio, and Wisconsin totaled 195, down from 461 in 1965.

What Happened?

As a result of these and other trends, the seven-day-a-week program church came on the scene to fill the vacuum left by the disappearance of the large Sunday morning churches. The new agendas of the liberal theology of the 1960s, 1970s, and 1980s did and do have a strong appeal to a large number of Americans, but most of them are not churchgoers. The evangelicals, moderates, and conservatives have moved in to reach and serve (1) the successors to those who were comfortable with the liberal theological agenda of the 1950s but are not attracted by either of the two newest agendas of the liberals, (2) that theologically more conservative generation born in the 1956–68 era, (3) the churchgoers of the 1950s who, as they grow older, seek a church with an agenda similar to what attracted them in the 1950s, and (4) people of all ages and various backgrounds who want more from their church than simply that Sunday morning schedule.

A significant number of pastors and churches affiliated with the mainline denominations have not abandoned the liberal theological position of the 1950s in favor of changing the world or saving the planet. They have adapted that 1950s liberal theological stance to today's world and created a distinctive version of the large seven-day-a-week full-service church that retains that intellectual approach to the faith but adds an experiential dimension to it. This is reinforced with superb biblical preaching, a heartwarming witness to the power of the gospel, respect for the dignity of the individual, a vigorous pursuit of excellence, a variety of opportunities for personal growth, a clear message of acceptance of the stranger, and various ministries of healing that are designed to help the broken become whole persons. These large and growing full-service churches have become the direct successors to the large liberal Sunday morning churches of the 1950s.

In addition, while they are only a fraction of the large church scene, scores of megachurches have emerged to serve one of these audiences: (1) that rapidly growing number of middle- and upper-class charismatic Christians; (2) those who are most comfortable with what is clearly a fundamentalist theological position (many of the older megachurches of today began with that constituency in the 1940s and 1950s); (3) people of all ages who are attracted by a combination of the liberal social agenda of the 1950s, meaningful and memorable preaching, an attractive seven-day-a-week program, and a strong teaching ministry; (4) those who seek a reconstructionist version of the faith; and (5) churchgoers who are convinced that the last days are drawing near with the close of the twentieth century. The new liberal agenda of the 1990s has little appeal to four of these five audiences.

Overlapping this change in the definition of a liberal theological stance is another issue that applies to congregations of all sizes. Why does one 250-member congregation average 400 at worship on Sunday morning while a few blocks away another 250-member church averages 85 at worship? Why does one 1,700-member parish average over 2,000 at worship while a few blocks away another 1,700-member parish averages 650?

The Power of Expectations

In both pairs of examples one part of the answer can be summarized in two words. Those key words are *expectations* and *commitment*. In some congregations a clear and consistent expectation is projected that everyone is expected to be in church every Sunday morning. Frequently that expectation is reinforced with the assumption that everyone will be in both Sunday school and worship every Sunday morning. Those expectations are part of the congregational culture that assumes a high level of commitment from every member. That assumption is reinforced by a highly redundant system. That high-commitment congregational culture projects high expectations in all expressions of stewardship, in the ministries with children, and in the qualifications required for volunteer leadership.

These high-commitment churches tend to be especially effective in reaching (1) providers of health-care services; (2) engineers, physicists, and others trained in the "hard" sciences; (3) adults born after 1955; (4) seekers on a religious pilgrimage; (5) adults who are comfortable with a life-style in which family, church, and job are the three major focal points of every week and who seek a full-service church with a seven-day-a-week program; (6) new Christians; (7) tithers; (8) "born again" Christians; (9) adults reared in a liberal church home; and (10) parents with strong upwardly mobile ambitions for their children. Many of the people who fit into one or more of those categories are comfortable in a large, complex, fast-paced, full-service, and numerically growing program church.

At the other end of this continuum are the low-commitment churches. Members are expected to attend Sunday morning worship on a few high holy days every year, plus whenever else it is convenient, to contribute a tiny percentage of their income to that congregation, and to take turns holding volunteer leadership positions. Few demands are placed on prospective new members. It is hoped that children will attend Sunday school, but they are not expected to be in worship for that entire hour. It is widely assumed that confirmation completes an obligation for youth and their parents that frees them from future demands on their time. The pastor assures visitors that everyone is welcome here, regardless of his or her belief system. Much of the weekday use of the building is to house events, activities, meetings, and programs owned and operated by other organizations. One of the models of the limited commitment parish is the pastor who is not expected to make a long-term commitment to this church and who is replaced every three or four years. The local time frame for planning is measured in weeks or months, not years. Most of today's low-commitment churches were established many decades earlier and now are experiencing three concurrent trends: (1) the level of commitment has been dropping for years, (2) the median age of the membership has been rising, and (3) the average attendance at worship has been dropping by an average of 1 or 2 percent annually for years.

Between these two points on that continuum are tens of thousands of Protestant churches, most of them founded before 1960, where the ratio of worship to membership runs between 45 and 65 percent. These are the churches that project a moderate level of expectations of the members. During the past decade the majority of them have been growing older and smaller.

While this generalization does not apply to all of today's large full-service churches, a majority of those founded since 1965 are located at the high commitment end of that continuum, and that is a significant reason for their continued numerical growth—but that is far from the only reason.

They Invite People to Come

Perhaps the most highly visible difference between the Sunday morning church and the full-service church is in how they spend their advertising dollars. The typical Sunday morning church purchases a weekly display advertisement in the local newspaper. It identifies the name and address of that congregation, lifts up the denominational affiliation, lists the names of the ordained ministers, and includes the Sunday schedule. Frequently the identical ad will be run for the entire year. It reinforces the image of this congregation as a Sunday morning church.

Today's full-service program church is more likely to allocate a larger percentage of the budget for advertising. Frequently a large share of that figure is spent on direct-mail advertising designed to invite the recipient to a particular weekday or evening event, program, activity, or group. These may range from an invitation to help pioneer a new Mothers' Club to participation in a new mutual support group or to enrollment in the upcoming Vacation Bible School.[7] The newspaper advertisement is changed weekly and often invites the reader to come to one specific event. This may be the new Saturday evening worship service or one of several Christmas Eve services or to enroll children in the early childhood development center or to come to a new Bible study series or a new parenting class. These ads reinforce the image of a full-service church. In addition, the full-service church may invest a portion of its advertising budget in television, radio, billboards, or the weekly free shopping guide. One way to grow is to invite people to come to your church.

Commitment, Missions, and Growth

Most of the very large and rapidly growing full-service churches place a high priority on missions. Typically in these churches 20 to 40 percent of total member contributions are allocated to missions and benevo-lences.

This raises four questions: Is this emphasis on missions one of the key factors behind the growth? Or does growth encourage a high priority for missions? Or is this emphasis on missions an essential component of the definition of a "full-service" church? Or does this high priority for missions encourage the evolution from a Sunday morning focus into seven-day-a-week programming?

The best answer to all four questions probably is yes. In other words, this is a chicken-and-egg set of questions. Placing a high priority on missions is highly compatible with the life-style of a large and rapidly growing full-service congregation. Likewise, lowering the priority on missions is compatible with cutting back on programming and placing a greater emphasis on the care of the members and the concerns of the staff as part of a larger design to reduce the size of what once was a large and numerically growing parish.

The Sinking Ship Syndrome

"I may not be the smartest man in the world," explained the seventy-year-old who recently left a congregation that had been shrinking at an average rate of 5 percent a year for over a decade to go to a flourishing seven-day-a-week program church, "but I know enough to get off the ship when everyone can see it's sinking. I was a member over at First Church for more than fifty years, and it was hard to leave, but I want to invest what time I have left as well as my energy and money in a church that has a future."

"The church we left after more than thirty years is trying to recreate 1953," reflected the woman. She and her husband, both in their late fifties, were among the new members at this rapidly growing megachurch. "Half of the pastor's sermons appeared to be designed to make the members feel guilty about not working harder to recreate the past."

"And the other half were designed to put me to sleep," interrupted her husband. "That guy is simply a dull preacher."

"Well, to make a long story short," continued the wife, "we decided that at our age we both needed a church that emphasized hope and love, and that's what we've found here."

"That's true," added the husband, "and we also wanted a church that has a future. Here we're among the oldest people in church on Sunday morning. Back there we were among the youngest.''

In the typical year, the baseball team that wins the pennant in the American League attracts a larger attendance than the teams that lose 60 percent or more of their games. Success attracts people.

While it is a secondary factor, one of the reasons the big program churches have become so large is that they have attracted substantial numbers of members of all ages who voted with their feet to leave the sinking ship in favor of the congregation that displays a strong future orientation and promises to be a safe harbor for the years ahead.

Once upon a time the marriage vow ''until death do us part'' was taken literally. That changed in the early 1960s, when the number of marriages in the United States that were terminated by divorce began to exceed the number ended by the death of a spouse. More than three out of five marriages that are now terminated in the United States end in divorce rather than death.

Likewise, while it was never stated this precisely, the vows of church membership assumed that this relationship would continue until terminated by death (sometimes that was the death of that congregation) or by a move by that member to a far-away residence. The majority of church members who change their place of residence in a given year still continue their membership in the same congregation.

For a growing number of church members, however, that relationship may be terminated today by (1) death of the member, (2) a move to a distant community, (3) the arrival of a new minister, (4) a change in the priorities of that congregation, (5) a change in the direction of the religious pilgrimage of the member, (6) immoral behavior by the pastor, (7) distrust of the administration of the finances of the church, (8) alienation created by denominational actions, (9) the decision by the parents to follow their adult children to another church, (10) the death of a spouse and remarriage, (11) an interdenominational or interfaith first marriage, or (12) following a friend to a different congregation.

In more specific terms, the most heavily traveled paths of today's church migrants are from (1) smaller to larger congregations; (2) dull preaching to lively and memorable preaching; (3) the Sunday morning church to the seven-day-a-week program church; (4) theologically liberal to theologically conservative churches; (5) numerically shrinking churches to numerically growing congregations; (6) non-directive styles of ministerial leadership to pastors who are able and willing to be initiating leaders; (7) churches with a weak teaching ministry to those with a strong teaching ministry; (8) old and long-established churches to new missions; (9) Roman Catholic to Protestant; (10) denominationally affiliated to nondenominational; (11) those with a high median age of the members to those with a low median age; (12) those with a limited ministry of music to those with a huge and varied ministry of music; (13) those that place a heavy reliance on verbal communication to those with a highly effective visualization of communication; (14) low quality to high quality; (15) the congregation in which the top priority is meeting the needs of the pastor to the congregation in which the top priority is responding to the religious and personal needs of the pilgrims, seekers, searchers, and others on a religious quest; (16) the self-centered parish to the mission-oriented congregation; (17) congregations torn by dissension to churches that have rallied behind unifying goals; (18) urban to non-metropolitan churches; (19) geographical parishes to regional churches; (20) non-charismatic to charismatic congregations; (21) connectional polity to congregational polity; (22) past- oriented or tradition-bound to future-oriented churches; (23) an emphasis on traditional church music to a focus on contemporary music; (24) member-oriented churches to outreach-oriented congregations; and (25) low-commitment to high-commitment churches.

Those are more than two dozen reasons why the big program churches are growing larger.

The Importance of Quality

One of the central selling points in recent years for automobiles, television sets, single-family homes, restaurants, and luxury hotels has been the word *quality*. The basic generalization for the churches today is this: the larger the size of the congregation, the less forgiving the people are for lapses in quality. This applies to the Sunday school, music, preaching, Vacation Bible School, the administration of the sacraments, the assimilation of new members, the ministries with teenagers, restrooms, off-street parking, meetings, financial management, the nursery, the bulletin boards, lighting, acoustics, the furniture, and internal communication.

The influence of kinship and friendship ties, shared experiences, tradition, intimacy, fellowship, denominational loyalties, one-to-one relationships, and humor often enables people in the smaller congregation to be very forgiving of low-quality performance.

One way that some churches become very large congregations and continue to attract large numbers of younger members is by attention to detail and to quality. This is a natural and compatible priority for the high-commitment churches described earlier. Almost every one of these churches that places a high priority on quality also includes members who are convinced this is an extravagant emphasis that offers the potential for financial savings. While rarely counted, these members usually are outnumbered by the newcomers who praise that attention to detail and emphasis on quality.

One example of this emphasis on quality that also is consistent with high commitment is the church that enlists only adults who have completed a teacher training program in staffing the Sunday school. A second is the church that reserves convenient parking for single mothers bringing children to the nursery. Another is the church that videotapes and critiques next Sunday's worship service as a part of the Thursday evening choir rehearsal. A fourth is the church that prepares a new display advertisement every week for the local newspaper. A fifth is the church that stations greeters wearing red blazers out in the parking lot every Sunday morning. When it rains, they carry red "loaner" umbrellas for those who come without one. A sixth is the church that delivers a loaf of home-baked bread or a pie or a cake by two o'clock Sunday afternoon to every first-time visitor that morning. A seventh is the church that has a team of volunteers who come in early Sunday morning to insert a half sheet of paper into every bulletin. These half-sheets are reproduced on the office copy machine early that morning to carry the latest news about persons who are hospitalized, new babies, deaths, and illnesses. An eighth is the church that stations a robed minister at every exit following each worship service so no one can leave without being greeted by a minister. Perhaps the most common example of attention to detail are the signs that make it easy for the first-time visitor to find a parking place, the right entrance into the building, and the way around the interior of what often is a complicated building.

Quality and attention to detail encourage many first-time visitors to return.

The Attractiveness of Choices

Another part of the explanation for the emergence of so many large congregations is the theme of this book. They are seven-day-a-week program churches. Another way of stating that can be summarized in the word *choices*. Because of the limitation of resources, one of which may be creativity, the vast majority of Protestant congregations on the North American continent offer people two choices: take it or leave it. "If you want to join us in the corporate worship of God, come when we gather, or don't come. If you want to sing in an adult choir or participate in a high school Sunday school class or share in an adult Bible study group, we offer only the one. Take it or leave it."

This is an especially significant factor in reaching and serving the generations born after World War II. Many of these persons grew up in a world that offered young people an unprecedented range of choices. When they shop for a new church home, they often pick a congregation that offers them a choice of both time and format in worship as well as a broad range of choices in other areas of programming and ministry. They also often choose the congregation that offers them choices in Sunday school. One church, for example, invites children from infants through age three to be in the nursery. Down the road a large full-service parish has one room for infants, another room for toddlers, a third room for children eighteen to twenty-four months old, a fourth room for those twenty-four to thirty months old, and a fifth room for children thirty to thirty-six months old. Which church do you think the mother of an eight-month-old or a twenty-one-month-old will choose?

The first church also may offer adults a choice from among three different adult classes, all scheduled for the same hour. The larger congregation may offer a choice of four adult classes during the first period on Sunday morning, seven during the second hour, and five during the third hour.

One result of this contemporary emphasis on choices, which is discouraging and disheartening news to leaders in smaller congregations with limited resources, can be summarized in an ancient four-word cliché: "Them that has gits." Those congregations with substantial discretionary resources are the ones most likely to be able to offer the attractive range of choices that enables them to reach large numbers of people born after 1955. The smaller congregations with limited resources

74

often see themselves growing older and smaller. The seven-day-a-week church is both a product and a beneficiary of this contemporary demand for a larger array of attractive choices.

What Do You Mean by "Community"?

The word *community* has now surpassed the word *first* when choosing the name for a new congregation. This represents one facet of the appeal of that word *community*.[8] In one way or another, nearly every Christian congregation on the North American continent today boasts about the feeling of community the members enjoy. The dream of some is that placing that magical word in the name will both reinforce the sense of community and also attract those seeking a supportive community of fellow believers.

One of the crucial differences between the typical Protestant congregation averaging sixty to a hundred at worship on Sunday morning and the growing full-service church that averages fourteen hundred at worship is in the operational implementation of that attractive word. The smaller church typically will conceptualize itself as a community of believers.

By contrast, the large and growing program church attracts younger newcomers for many reasons, several of which have been identified earlier in this chapter. Another is that the leaders, both paid and volunteer, conceptualize this huge collection of people, not as one community, but rather as a community of communities. These sub-communities may include various choirs, adult Sunday school classes, four to ten different youth groups, a variety of circles in the women's organization, Bible study groups, and mutual support communities built around a common theme. The smaller communities may include a dozen or fewer participants, while the largest may attract a couple of hundred active members.

One fringe benefit is that this enables those who seek the intimacy and fellowship of a small church, but also enjoy the range of choices available only in the large seven-day-a-week parish, to have their cake and eat it, too.

Far more important in explaining the rapid growth of some of the very large churches of today is the quality of those communities. One expression of community that is highly valued by tens of thousands of today's parents often is found in the seven-day-a-week church that offers a supportive, yet challenging, environment for children. That environment has been designed to affirm and reinforce such traditional values as honesty, self-reliance, deferred gratification, helping those in need, initiative, hard work, punctuality, creativity, neighbor-centered love, trust, cooperation, ethical behavior, traditional moral values, responsibility for the consequences of one's actions, and respect for other people as well as academic skills. This is usually a highly structured environment that may include a Christian day school as well as other activities and programs.[9] This environment possesses a special appeal to thousands of single-parent mothers who seek a supportive community for the rearing of children.

Several decades ago the most influential socializing forces in the life of the majority of children included parents, siblings, kinfolks, church, the school, teachers, Sunday school, radio, motion pictures, newspapers, magazines, patriotism (especially for those born between 1910 and 1935), and voluntary associations such as Scouting, 4H Clubs, and similar adult-managed groups. Most of these sought to transmit to the next generation a common standard of ethical behavior and moral values.

Many of today's children and youth are heavily influenced by peer groups, television, the part-time job, motion pictures, the shopping mall, MTV, gangs, law enforcement, and the "youth culture."

These churches are seeking to create a community in which adult Christians will have the opportunity to model for that group of children and youth a Christian set of moral values and ethical behavior. The larger the number of restrictions placed on the public schools in transmitting traditional moral values and standards of ethical behavior, the greater the appeal of these Christian day schools—especially to parents employed in very large public school systems.

Another expression of community in many seven-day-a-week churches can be seen in the growing number of mutual support groups found in these program churches.

Perhaps the most highly visible expression of community in scores of megachurches serving large numbers of retirees are the groups designed for the new empty nesters, the recently widowed, the newly retired person who feels lost without a regular job, or the parents who recently discovered an adult child is gay or lesbian. One of the most interesting expressions of community within this generation consists of volunteers who commit several weeks a year to assisting in the construction of buildings for new congregations or improvements to the facilities at a church camp or repairing the damage following a hurricane or tornado or flood or earthquake. As these mature adults work and live together week after week, a deep sense of community emerges.

The range of choices the full-service program church offers people in search of Christian community is one of the most powerful factors behind the rapid growth of hundreds of today's large full-service churches.

Governance, Goals, and Consequences

What do American agriculture, the absentee ownership of newspapers, public schools in the large central cities, and public housing have in common?

All four demonstrate the unfortunate impact on people when the formulation of long-range policies and the making of critical decisions is geographically separated from the place where the consequences of those policies and decisions will be felt.

A parallel generalization is that denominational priorities and goals are not an adequate substitute for local visionary leadership.

These two generalizations introduce another reason behind the recent rapid growth of the large full-service churches. The extensive range of choices that is a feature of the huge program church almost by definition is a product of three factors. The first is an exceptional sensitivity to the contemporary religious and personal needs of the people that congregation is seeking to reach and serve. The second is the motivation of a locally inspired and locally supported vision of how this church can be responsive to those needs. The third is that the policy and program decisions required for the implementation of that vision are made locally, where the consequences will be felt.

This last paragraph offers a partial explanation for the growing number of large seven-day-a-week churches. It offers a partial explanation for the disproportionately large number of independent and nondenominational megachurches. This last paragraph also offers a partial explanation for the fact that the proportion of United Methodist congregations averaging over seven hundred at worship is only one-sixth of what it is for the rest of American Protestantism.

This explanation also creates considerable discomfort among those people, such as this writer, who have been longtime proponents of greater inter-congregational cooperation, who advocate the interdependence of churches, who worry about accountability, and who take seriously the doctrine of original sin.

Regardless of one's own feelings, inherited values, and preferences, this part of the explanation for the growth of seven-day-a-week churches also helps us to understand several other contemporary trends. It helps to explain the great interest in governance in so many of today's large congregations. (See chapter 5.) It helps to explain why a rapidly growing number of the emerging full-service parishes are turning to mega-churches, rather than to denominational headquarters or to theological seminaries, for models, ideas, the training of program staff, printed materials, videotapes, the continuing education of volunteer leaders, music, associate ministers, and "how-to" books. These generalizations also offer a partial explanation for the fact that a disproportionately large number of the churchgoers born after World War II are choosing congregations that are completely self-governing institutions. These younger generations display considerable skepticism toward "outside" authority figures. As a group, they strongly prefer local control of the institutions that affect their lives.

Tradition Bound or Market Driven?

"It is extremely important that at some time during your visit you ask these five questions," pleaded the minister of parish life in a large and rapidly growing congregation. She was addressing a group of thirty volunteers who were preparing to call on the class of new members who had joined the previous Sunday.

"First, we want to know why they came here the first time. What brought them?" continued this staff person as she passed out 3" by 5" cards with the questions printed on them. "We need to know what appealed to them. Second, find out why they came back a second time. That may be a completely different reason from why they originally came. Third, ask them what they like best about this church today. These are new members, and we need to know what newcomers think about what we do best."

"You don't expect us to remember all these answers, do you?" challenged one volunteer. "I have four addresses on my list that include eleven people. Am I supposed to get one answer per house or one answer for each question from each new member?''

"First, write down the responses,'' urged the minister of parish life. "People are flattered when they see you place such importance on what they say that you write it down. Second, yes, we would like to secure a response to each question from each new member. Everyone's opinion is important! We realize that may not always be possible. For example, one of your calls may be on a home with a mother, father, and two older teenagers. You may not find all four at home when you call, but please try.''

"What are the other two questions?'' called out an impatient volunteer.

"The fourth is to ask what they would like to see added, changed, deleted, expanded, or strengthened in our present program,'' quickly responded the staffer. "The fifth, which is the most subjective, is to inquire about how well they feel they have been assimilated into our fellowship and then to discover how we can facilitate their assimilation.''[10]

In another church not too many miles away, a different group of volunteers were being instructed on how to call on the people who had united with that congregation on the previous Sunday.

"The heart of your assignment consists of three parts. First, deliver a box of offering envelopes and try to get them to fill out a pledge card for the balance of this year,'' declared the person in charge. "Second, Mrs. Jackson has resigned as teacher of our third- and fourth-grade Sunday school class effective the last Sunday of this month. If any of you meet someone who could replace her, call me as soon as you get home.''

"Be sure to let our choir director know if you run into any tenors,'' interrupted a volunteer who also sang in the choir. "We're down to two tenors, and one of them is absent a lot.''

"Third,'' resumed the person giving out the instructions, "please be sure to ask everyone to fill out this time and talent inventory. That will be of great help to our nominating committee when it meets this fall. Lest there be any misunderstanding, Mike Lawson, who chairs our finance committee, told me we need at least $9,500 in pledges from this class of new members if we are to finish the year in the black. As you probably know, our biggest contributor died last spring, and two other big contributors will be moving to New Mexico in a couple of months.''

These two vignettes help to explain why some churches continue to attract large numbers of new people, but they also help to explain the differences between two groups of churches.

The Tradition-Bound Majority

The vast majority of the Protestant congregations on the North American continent are heavily influenced by tradition, survival goals, customs, past precedents, history, and their own institutional culture.

Unless a new and powerful force is introduced into the equation, the standard expectation is that tomorrow will resemble today. The beginning point for preparing next year's budget is this year's budget or how to respond to unanticipated repairs to this sacred building. The comparison base for evaluating the new pastor is the personality, performance, and gifts of the previous minister. The criterion for deciding on the number of bulletins to be reproduced for next Sunday's worship service is the number used last Sunday, perhaps with a look at the number required for the equivalent Sunday last year. The evaluation of the size of the current youth group will be a comparison with last year's numbers. The beginning point for a recommendation for the minister's compensation for next year will be this year's compensation. The assignment of rooms to Sunday school classes will begin with past use.

Even more significant is the strong member orientation of these churches. The top priority on the pastor's time is assumed to be the care of today's members. The Sunday morning schedule is determined by the preferences of the members in general and the volunteer leaders in particular. The Sunday morning worship experience is designed to meet the needs of believers in general and today's members in particular. The ministries with teenagers usually are designed and scheduled with the hope of serving the children of today's members.

In some congregations this strong member orientation prohibits the pastor from officiating at a wedding in which neither party is a member of the church or from conducting the funeral service for a non-member. In other congregations this strong member orientation often means that special events, such as the Christmas Eve services or Thanksgiving morning service or Saturday evening worship, are designed, scheduled, and publicized on the assumption that these are for the benefit of members. The total ministry of music, the choices of hymns, and the liturgy often are chosen to please today's members. Occasionally one of the motivations for seeking to attract more new members is the hope that they will reduce the financial burden on the dwindling number of current members and/or will be a source of new teachers, choir members, and workers.

In some congregations this powerful member orientation is altered by the influence of outside factors that shape the life and ministry of these churches. The most highly visible examples are theological seminaries, continuing education events for both the laity and the clergy, the denominational committee that created a new hymnal, the lectionary, denominational mergers, the system for ministerial placement, and various denominationally initiated priorities.

The most highly visible consequence of this strong member orientation is that it facilitates the process of growing older and smaller. The stronger the pressures of tradition and the greater the member orientation, the more likely that the congregation will shrink in numbers as the members grow older.

The Market-Driven Minority

By contrast, a small but rapidly growing number of churches are driven by a desire to reach, attract, and serve new generations of youth and adults. In a few extreme examples, the Sunday morning worship experience is designed for seekers, persons on a religious pilgrimage, skeptics, inquirers, first-time visitors, and searchers. The worship service designed for the committed Christians is scheduled for another time during the week.

Almost by definition the full-service program church fits into this category of market-driven congregations. That is why it is a seven-day-a-week parish, rather than a Sunday morning church. That orientation explains why those volunteers calling on new members in the first vignette were instructed to ask that set of questions, rather than to concentrate on how the new members could help implement the survival goals of the congregation. This market orientation helps to explain why so many seven-day-a-week churches are growing so large.

This sensitivity to the market also explains some of the criticisms from those who are convinced that obedience to God and faithfulness to the gospel are undermined whenever the church becomes excessively concerned with the agendas the people bring with them. This tension is highly visible today in the American Catholic Church.[11] Which should be given the higher priority in formulating long-range policies and in the allocation of scarce resources? Tradition? Institutional survival goals? The desires of today's members? The religious and personal needs of people not involved in the life of any worshiping community? The poor? The oppressed? The value systems of those who have been elected or appointed to influential ecclesiastical offices?

Should the churches expect people to be responsive to the agenda prepared by the church? Or should the churches seek to discover and be responsive to the agendas the people bring with them? That is the issue in a highly divisive debate in American Protestantism as well as in American Catholicism!

The basic distinction between these two approaches to the world is described in an award-winning book, *Innovation in Marketing,* by Theodore Levitt.[12] This book—which was written for a business, not a church, audience—lifts up the difference between focusing on the needs of the seller rather than on the needs of the buyer. Levitt urges the reader to concentrate on the needs of the people, rather than on the needs of the institution. Literally scores of books and influential articles have been published during the past three decades by other authors who emphasize this same point. This perspective calls for focusing on the consumer of the services or program, not on the producer's needs.[13]

The most highly visible example of this distinction in the churches can be seen in the advertisements on the church page of the Friday or Saturday newspapers. In most newspapers the vast majority of these ads resemble the "tombstone" notice run by a stockbroker announcing a new bond issue or the sale of new stock in a company. This satisfies certain legal requirements. The parallel is the ad run by a church that announces the name and address of a particular congregation plus the Sunday schedule and the names of the staff. It may include the text and title for Sunday's sermon. That satisfies those who contend, "We should advertise our church in the newspaper."

Once in a while, however, that same page will carry the church ad that is addressed to the needs of the reader. Relatively few of the words in these ads relate to the advertiser. Most of the words are directed to the religious pilgrimage and needs of the reader.

A second example of this market-driven approach surfaced back in the

1960s when dozens of congregations made the changes necessary to attract and welcome the so-called Jesus People. Among the most common of these changes was a willingness to relax the dress code, to expand the Sunday schedule, to accept different music, to double or triple the number of worshipers, to enlarge the teaching ministry, and to add new staff members to serve the increased numbers.

A third example is in those denominations willing to create new congregations to reach and serve the waves of immigrants from Central and South America and the Pacific Rim. This usually required postponing the dream of integrating all immigrants into Anglo churches, changes in the requirements for ministerial standing, and multilingual publications.

A fourth example is in new church development directed at younger generations of the population. This usually has meant abandoning the traditional approaches to ministerial training, ordination, and placement; accepting and utilizing new approaches to new-member enlistment; creating a different format for corporate worship; dropping the old pattern of beginning small in the hope of growing larger in favor of beginning large; offering very modest or no financial subsidies; emphasizing a far greater sensitivity to the needs of people and less dependence on denominational or institutional loyalties; affirming a greater recognition of the power of excellent preaching and top-quality oral communication; and offering prospective members meaningful choices.

The fifth example, which is the theme of this book, is the seven-day-a-week church.

The sixth example of the operational expression of this division between the tradition-oriented churches and the market-driven churches is television. Television is a superb marketing tool for those seeking to reach people beyond a local audience. Television has turned out to be an exceptionally powerful tool for marketing professional sports, automobiles, medicines, home appliances, American history, wars, music, exercise, diet, clothing, toys, violence, a common national language and accent, political candidates, and toothpaste. Television has not been effective in marketing institutions (political parties, corporations, denominations), books, abstract concepts (peace, brotherhood, civility, grace, moral values, ethical behavior, deferred gratification), reading, writing, or spelling.

Television, unlike the printed word, does not have centuries of tradition behind it to reinforce its value. Thus it should surprise no one that those who place a high value on tradition and on the typographic page[14] rarely turn to television to proclaim the Gospel, while the market-driven churches find television to be a useful tool.

Likewise it is internally consistent for newspaper advertisements created by the tradition-bound churches to focus on the institutional affiliation, the Sunday morning schedule, and the sermon title chosen by the preacher of the week. This is what our tradition has to offer. Occasionally this institutional self-identification is reinforced by a line drawing of the church building and the decision to run the identical ad week after week. In a few cases all congregations affiliated with the same religious tradition will run their weekly newspaper ad in one long box.

As was pointed out earlier, it also is internally consistent for the market-driven church to use a redundant advertising system that includes direct mail, newspaper ads, radio spots, television, and billboards, each of which carries messages directed at the religious or personal concerns of the reader, viewer, or listener. Instead of promoting their institution, these market-driven churches concentrate on identifying and responding to the agendas of the people.

Perhaps the most widely resented lesson that television has taught is that the responsibility for grabbing and holding the attention of people rests on the communicator, not on the listeners, viewers, or readers. Tradition taught that churchgoers are expected to remain alert, listen to the sermon and ingest it into their hearts, souls, minds, and being. Authors have depended on the hope that when a person makes a substantial financial investment in purchasing a book, that allocation of scarce resources will motivate the buyer to read that book. The coming of the affluent society has been accompanied by the fact that today more books are sold than are read. Thus the responsibility is now largely on the author to secure and maintain the interest of the reader. Many people read only a chapter or two from a particular book. This means that each chapter has to be able to command the attention of the reader. That also is one explanation for the repetition that enables each chapter to stand alone as one complete unit. The parallel is that some people go to Sunday school in Church A, worship on Sunday evening in Church B, and work as a volunteer in an outreach ministry sponsored by Church C.

Today's market-driven churches recognize and accept this as a simple fact of life. The tradition-bound congregations often are filled with "oughts" on how people ought to respond and therefore do not make the effort necessary to grab and hold people's attention. The safe operational assumption is that the younger the audience a congregation is seeking to reach and serve, the larger the share of the responsibility it must carry in effective two-way communication.

Which Marketing Strategy?

"Back when my wife and I joined this congregation in 1979, it was still a growing church," recalled Chuck Allen, an influential member of the finance committee at Good Shepherd Church. "For the past five years, however, our numbers have been shrinking. I'm convinced the time has come to reverse that and the best way to do it is by spending more money on advertising. My wife and I are prepared to increase our pledge by $500 if the rest of you are willing to set aside $5,000 in the budget for advertising for this coming year."

The ensuing discussion could be summarized by five questions. Would the results justify the expenditure? Where would they find the other $4,500? What percentage of the total budget should be allocated to advertising? Were there not other urgent needs that should rank ahead of advertising in setting the priorities for next year's budget? Would this set a dangerous precedent?

These are interesting questions, but all are of secondary importance. When the subject of reversing a period of numerical decline or of church growth comes up, every congregation is limited to five alternatives, no more, no less. These five alternatives offer a better beginning point when the question of how to spend those advertising dollars is raised.

The first alternative, and the one preferred by many parishioners, is to grow your own replacements. In simple terms this might mean the husband-wife couple with three young children eventually will be replaced by six adults, those three children plus their spouses.

This is simple biological growth combined with the expectation that the congregation not only will be able to retain the allegiance of all the children from member families, but also will attract the spouses of all who marry non-members. In today's world that may be an extravagant expectation. In marketing terms it means growing your own future constituency or maintaining your current market.

A second alternative is to seek to reach more of the people who resemble the present membership. In church-growth terminology that often is referred to as the homogeneous unit principle. Birds of a feather do tend to flock together, and the easiest road to numerical growth is to focus on the strengths and assets of this particular congregation and seek to attract more people from that slice of the population now being served. Thus if a congregation today is composed largely of third- or fourth-generation white Anglo-Americans born before 1930, one alternative is to expand the outreach by attracting more of that generation. In marketing terms this often is called market penetration. The goal is to reach more of that slice of the population now being served.

One of the attractive features of this strategy is that it requires few changes. In general terms implementation requires improving the quality of the current programs and ministries and perhaps expanding the physical facilities. For a majority of congregations this alternative also will require expanding the radius of the service area from two or three miles to six to fifteen miles. That usually requires more off-street parking. "More of the same, only better" can be the operational slogan for implementing this alternative. This second marketing strategy has great appeal to the Sunday morning church. "Rather than change, let's seek to draw people from a larger piece of geography."

By contrast, the next three alternatives usually require substantial changes. Opposition to these changes may make it difficult to implement any of them. The first, and usually the least threatening of the three, is to expand that slice of the market now being served.

For the smaller congregations in which the three most powerful cohesive ties are parents and siblings, marriage, and friendships, this may mean identifying and attracting people who are total strangers and who are not related to today's members. That almost certainly will require improving and expanding the present system of new-member enlistment, and it may require other changes.

For the congregation that averages eighty-five at worship in a room that will comfortably seat fewer than one hundred, this probably will require adding a second worship experience on Sunday morning. For others, the choice of this alternative may require remodeling or enlarging the educational facilities or adding more off-street parking or enlarging the paid staff in order to serve more people. This third strategy of expanding the slice of the market to be served also is a favorite of many

Sunday morning churches and usually is more effective than the previous strategy of expanding the geographical area to be served.

These efforts to expand the size of the market served by this congregation mean a broader audience, greater complexity, higher unit dollar costs, increased anonymity, and, usually, an improvement in the quality of the physical facilities. Spending more money, however, does not guarantee a larger constituency.

A fourth alternative is one that has been followed by scores of Sunday morning churches that have transformed themselves into seven-day-a-week parishes. It requires substantial changes and is what experts in marketing describe as product development. This means adding new and attractive products to what you offer your customers. From the perspective of your church this may be adding a weekday pre-kindergarten program to your educational ministry or organizing a new high school youth choir or adding new and different approaches to Bible study or creating a new ministry with young adults or developing a ministry with single, formerly married adults or offering a mutual support group for the adult children of alcoholic parents or adding a Saturday evening worship service to your present schedule or developing a package of specialized ministries with retirees or beginning the Sunday morning schedule with breakfast or sponsoring annual trips to the Holy Land or beginning an adult day-care center.

The central point is to reach and serve a larger slice of the total population by spreading the total program through the entire week, thus making room in the schedule to add a variety of new ministries, classes, programs, groups, and activities.[15] As a result the Sunday morning church is transformed into a seven-day-a-week parish. Obviously this requires additional resources, including skilled and dedicated volunteers, physical facilities, expert leadership, money, and creativity. Thus it is easy to understand why this marketing strategy often has greater appeal to the larger churches.

The final alternative is often described simply as diversification. It is a combination of the last two—expanding the market and product development.

For many full-service parishes this really is the final stage in their evolution, which has been made possible by expanding beyond that Sunday morning focus. One example is the Anglo congregation that schedules a full worship experience in Korean early Sunday afternoon, a

Spanish-language service Sunday evening, a prayer-and-praise service on Tuesday evening, English-as-a-second-language classes on five mornings and five evenings every week, a service of intercessory prayer every Wednesday evening, a Mothers' Club every Thursday morning, an early childhood development center that is open five mornings a week, and a peace vigil every Friday evening.

Another example of diversification is the congregation composed largely of members born before 1935 that creates a new and different worship experience designed by and for people born after 1955. A third is the women's organization that continues its historic emphasis on missions, but adds one new circle for first-time mothers, a second new circle for young widowed women, a third new circle organized around arts and crafts, a fourth new circle that is an advocacy group on the issue of world hunger, a fifth new circle created to be a support group for the nearby seminary library, and a sixth new circle for single mothers.

The broad generalization is that Sunday morning churches tend to use one of the first three of these five marketing strategies while the seven-day-a-week parish follows the fourth or fifth. These differences in marketing strategies also help to explain why so many of the seven-day-a-week churches have grown so large.

Count the Entry Points

Another part of the explanation for the size and rapid growth of many of today's full-service churches is a product of several factors. One is the fact they are seven-day-a-week program churches. Another is their size. A third is their focus on the religious needs of people. This can be illustrated by comparing two types of congregations.

The first includes the majority of long-established churches. Frequently they resemble a large closed circle. Most of the resources are allocated to meeting the needs of the members already within that circle. This includes the priorities on the pastor's time and energy, the use of the building, the nature of the organizational life such as the Sunday school, the ministry of music, the women's organization, the priorities in the expenditures of money, the use of the time contributed by volunteers, and the dominant approach to ministry.

If that congregation is to grow in numbers, it probably will be necessary to change the nature of that closed circle. One means of accomplishing that may be to bring in a new pastor who will introduce a new and different approach to ministry, attract new people, change the style of congregational life, alienate at least a few of the longtime members, and transform the culture of that congregation. Pastors who can accomplish that are comparatively rare! Far more often the culture of that congregation turns out to be more powerful and molds the newly arrived minister to fit the tradition, style, ethos, approach to ministry, schedule, goals, priorities, and values of that congregation.

Thus most of these congregations count themselves fortunate whenever the number of new members received in any one year equals the number who leave. The number of attractive entry points where newcomers will find their religious and personal needs are being met is too few for that congregation to grow in numbers. One reason, of course, is that after the needs and expectations of the members are met and fulfilled, insufficient discretionary resources (time, volunteers, creativity, money, space, etc.) remain to create those additional entry points for potential newcomers.

The second type of congregation has deliberately, skillfully, and intentionally created a broad range of entry points for newcomers. This deliberate effort to create additional entry points for newcomers is compatible with that seven-day-a-week schedule, with that "product development" or "diversification" approach to marketing described earlier, and with the role of the senior pastor as initiating leader.[16] Furthermore the decision to expand the number of entry points is facilitated by the resources the large congregation can mobilize.

While this may sound harsh, the congregation that is content to grow older and smaller usually finds it easy to rationalize reducing the number and variety of entry points for potential future new members. This course of action can be defended on a variety of grounds, including efficiency, economy, a reduction in complexity, a simpler schedule, and convenience.

By contrast, the decision to increase the number and variety of entry points is like making water run uphill. It can be done, and we know how to do it, but it requires creativity, persistence, an affirmation of complexity, additional resources, ingenuity, a willingness to live with charges of extravagance, and resisting the temptation to relax and let nature take its course. The natural tendency is for water to run downhill, for older institutions to place comfort and tradition at the top of the

THE SEVEN-DAY-A-WEEK CHURCH

priority list, and for long-established Protestant congregations to grow older and smaller.

What Is Your Definition of Ministry?

Perhaps the most subtle, but certainly one of the most powerful, reasons for the continued numerical growth of the large full-service churches lies in the definition of ministry. This can be illustrated by looking at two types of churches in nearly any large central city.

The more common of the two is the long-established Protestant congregation that has been affected by population changes. The traditional Anglo constituency has decreased in numbers. Many have moved away, others have died, and a small number are homebound. Efforts to reach the new residents, who represent a different ethnic, racial, national, lingual, or social class slice of the population produce few replacement members. The pastor, a few of the most active members, and denominational leaders are determined to continue a "Christian presence" in this neighborhood. The historic priorities on corporate worship, the teaching ministry, and the supportive community are expanded to include a variety of direct service social welfare ministries.

This sequence was especially common in the 1880s, the 1920s, and the 1960s. In the 1960s a new component was added to what now was often described as "urban ministries." This new component was to become an aggressive advocate on behalf of the poor, the oppressed, the downtrodden, the victims of injustice, the unemployed, the homeless, the hungry, and the single-parent family.

During the 1960s the financial base for urban ministries often was enhanced by governmental resources as well as gifts from suburban churches and denominational grants. As the years rolled by, however, the combination of inflation, the erosion of subsidies, and a continued decline in the membership resulted in a shortage of resources. The clientele for the direct services of the social welfare ministries often grew as fewer and fewer people participated in corporate worship or the teaching ministry or congregational life. When the 1990s brought another surge of interest in "urban ministries," this often was conceptualized as centering on advocacy and/or social welfare services. The goal was and is to help those who need help.

Far less common is the definition of "urban ministry" in the large and growing full-service church. The beginning point in these churches is not help but transformation. This definition of ministry is based on the assumption, as was pointed out earlier, that the Gospel of Jesus Christ has the power to transform the life of an individual. Typically this is reinforced by a variety of supportive programs that include direct social services, but that is not the beginning point for defining ministry.

This definition of urban ministries places corporate worship at the center of the design with a close second being the creation of caring communities within the larger fellowship. The teaching ministry is a close third. The teaching ministry includes a strong emphasis on leadership development. Direct social services and advocacy ministries are not ignored, but they are not at the center of this definition of urban ministries.

As people discover that their own lives have been transformed by the power of the Gospel, they bring others. That is the number-one reason these churches attract an endless stream of newcomers. This takes us back to a point made earlier. When the top priority of any one congregation is on changing the world or on saving the planet, relatively few respond. When the top priority is the transformation of the lives of individuals by the power of the Gospel, the Andrews of today bring their brothers and sisters (see John 1:40).

CHAPTER FOUR

Staffing the Full-Service Church

T he first characteristic we look for as we add staff is competence,'' declared the senior minister of one large full-service church. ''Our theme is excellence, and that requires exceptionally competent staff. Once we begin to compromise the quality of our ministry, we'll be history.''

''I'm on the team that interviews the final candidates for every program position we fill,'' explained a volunteer leader from another large and rapidly growing program church. ''I look for signs of Christian commitment, the sense of a special calling to a Christian vocation, a high level of spirituality, a strong and unapologetic prayer life, and expressions of self-discipline. We can teach skills, and we can instill a desire for competence, but we don't have time to convert the unconverted.''

''We've learned from experience that the crucial variable for us is character,'' reflected the executive pastor of a very large and rapidly growing independent church. ''The only occasions we have regretted hiring someone was when we slipped up on the issue of character. For us, character is number one, and everything else is secondary.''

''We conceptualize the program staff as a team, and so our first question in evaluating candidates is simple. Is this someone who will fit into our team?'' offered the program director of another seven-day-a-week church. ''In smaller churches it may be possible for each staff person to preside over a semi-autonomous fiefdom, but we look at our total ministry as one large, coherent, internally consistent, and carefully designed package, not as a collection of unrelated independent little kingdoms. That's why all of our program staff have to see themselves as members of the same team."

* * * *

These reflections, all of which are close to verbatim comments from the sources indicated, provide one approach to staffing. All the characteristics and qualities identified are important. A different approach, and the one followed most frequently, usually begins with the focus on *do*, not *are*. Rather than beginning by identifying the critical qualities or characteristics, this approach begins by looking at what a staff member will do.

One course of action that is consistent with this functional approach can be summarized in a long sentence. The large-program church needs a senior minister who is a superb preacher and a visionary, initiating leader who resells "the vision" several times a year; an executive pastor who can manage the institution; and a program director who can create, staff, and oversee a seven-day-a-week program. Add to that troika a specialist in music who can create and oversee a large ministry of music that also is supportive of both worship and the group life, and that is a good beginning point. Those four responsibilities are of critical importance.

What Is Not Getting Done Now?

Frequently, however, the beginning point is not a completely blank slate but a congregation that already has a senior minister plus other paid staff members. Thus the congregation that is seeking to move in the direction of becoming a full-service church must begin with the status quo. In this situation a useful question is this: "What is not getting done now, because we are not staffed to make that happen, that we must do in order to become an attractive seven-day-a-week church?"

The obvious beginning point is worship and preaching. A simple way to evaluate that is to ask, "Is our average attendance at worship increasing by at least 10 percent annually?" If the answer is in the affirmative, the wisest course of action may be to move to the next question.

For the majority of churches, however, a better beginning question is "Are we offering the range of choices in worship and preaching that is consistent with our role as a full-service church?'' This may lead to adding another excellent preacher and/or a creative worship leader to the staff. In other churches this may lead to broadening and enlarging the ministry of music.

What Is Good Preaching?

At this point it may be appropriate to inject a word about the content of the preaching. Many critics of the megachurches denounce the content of the sermons with comments such as these: ''They're filled with fluff''; ''It's feel good religion''; ''They completely ignore sin''; ''They overemphasize the power of positive thinking''; or ''They're too patriotic and nationalistic.''

These and similar criticisms greatly oversimplify a complex issue. It is true that in many of the megachurches most of the sermons could be classified in one of six categories: (1) God loves you and how you can love the Lord with all your heart, mind, and soul; (2) how to get from Monday to Friday by following Christ; (3) teaching sermons on the basic beliefs of Christianity designed for newcomers to the faith and adults who did not learn much about the faith when they were children; (4) what the Bible says about a specific problem the listener brought to church today; (5) how Christians bear one another's burdens; and (6) the transformational power of the Gospel for those who accept Jesus Christ as Lord and Savior.

With the possible exception of the last category, many of the sermons preached in numerically declining churches could be placed in one of these categories. The crucial distinction between the preaching in the numerically growing churches and those that are shrinking in size is not in the message. The crucial difference is in the messenger. The sermons in the numerically growing churches are delivered in a manner that is convincing, coherent, persuasive, and clear. The listener identifies with the illustrations, finds the content to be meaningful, and leaves feeling, ''I have heard something that enriches and strengthens my faith.'' The delivery, not the content, causes the listener to describe these sermons as ''memorable,'' ''relevant,'' and ''credible.'' The sermon is credible because the hearer is convinced that the preacher deeply believes what he or she is saying. Simple sincerity does not always produce credibility. The transformational power of the Gospel is communicated less by the words that are spoken and more by the obvious fact that the life of that preacher has been transformed by Jesus Christ. That witness is more compelling than the words. In transformational preaching, the message, as Marshall McLuhan told us thirty years ago, is the medium.

Are You Reaching All of Your Audiences?

A different beginning point for a discussion about staffing is appropriate in congregations that reach far more people with their weekday program than they do on Sunday morning. This often means staffing to broaden the range of choices in worship and preaching. One increasingly common example of that is the parish that offers an informal Saturday evening service designed to reach three or four overlapping audiences. These audiences may include (1) people who work on Sunday; (2) people who work the night shift, come to worship before leaving for work, and go from work to bed; (3) those who want all day Sunday free to visit relatives or take trips or sleep late; (4) empty-nest couples who find Saturday evening to be a lonely period now that the youngest child has left home; (5) some of those two to seven million church members who regularly participate in worship at two or more congregations every week; (6) couples in an interfaith marriage that calls for both to go to Mass at a Roman Catholic parish on Sunday morning; (7) newcomers to the community who are church shopping; (8) adults who prefer a smaller congregation to the bigger crowds on Sunday morning; (9) young couples who seek a worship experience, warm fellowship, and a learning experience in one package; (10) the committed volunteers who have decided to help make the Saturday evening "experiment" a success and who know they are needed; (11) those who are attracted by that particular type or style of worship; (12) older adults who live alone; (13) longtime members who can remember "back when everyone here knew everyone else, and now it's just a big anonymous crowd on Sunday mornings"; (14) men who no longer own a necktie and/or women who are more comfortable in a pantsuit or slacks or shorts than in a skirt or dress; (15) people who prefer the hymns used in the Saturday evening service to those scheduled for Sunday morning; (16) the greeters, ushers, and choir members who are necessary for that Saturday evening service; (17) young adults (typically age seventeen to twenty-five) who prefer a worship experience in which they have a high level of ownership; (18)

young divorced or widowed mothers who find the Saturday evening schedule more appealing than the Sunday morning program; (19) those who are more comfortable with the leisurely pace of the Saturday evening schedule than with the hurried Sunday morning atmosphere; (20) that large, specialized ministry with formerly married and never-married young adults who have adopted Saturday evening as their meeting night and either begin or conclude the evening with worship; (21) a group who prefer a language other than English for worship; (22) working-class adults who would not be comfortable in the Sunday morning service designed for upper middle class adults;[1] and (23) those who look forward to the Saturday evening that begins with a leisurely meal, followed by worship, an adult class, fellowship, dessert, and a 10:30 dismissal.

After it is decided which of these audiences the Saturday evening service(s) should be designed to reach and serve, the appropriate staffing decisions can be made.

The Sunday morning schedule may include an early service centered on Holy Communion, with the minister of pastoral care preaching on forty Sundays a year and the senior minister preaching once a month. This may be followed by two concurrent services. Typically one is a traditional, formal, and liturgical experience in the sanctuary while several hundred worship in the fellowship hall at the same hour in an informal service with contemporary music and a different style of preaching. The last service of the weekend follows and may be designed for an audience that comes largely from a different religious tradition or has had no previous church affiliation and includes many visitors.

This range of choices is consistent with the goal of reaching and serving a highly diverse or pluralistic collection of people. Incidentally, this schedule illustrates one of the biggest differences between the Sunday morning church and the full-service program parish. Typically the Sunday morning church is designed to reach only two or three slices from the local population. That means it is internally consistent to offer two worship services on Sunday with the second being a carbon copy of the first. In some extreme cases the same bulletin is used at both services and the same adult choir sings the same anthem at both services. By contrast, the range of five *different* worship experiences described earlier is designed to offer a meaningful worship experience to a broad range of people.

This also means that the homogeneous principle of church growth often is relevant to the plans of the Sunday morning church, but is less relevant to the full-service program church seeking to serve a large and diverse collection of people.

What Does Our Senior Minister Do Best?

Staffing for worship naturally is the first priority. A second priority question is in response to a more subjective issue. Every senior minister has both strengths and weaknesses, but more particularly, is limited to 168 hours a week. One way to state it is "What does our senior minister do best, and how can we staff this congregation to take advantage of the strengths and assets of our senior minister?" A better way may be to ask, "What will our senior minister not do in order to concentrate time and energy on those things our senior minister does best?"

Among the most common functions senior ministers in numerically growing full-service churches delegate to others are (1) administration and overseeing the institution; (2) oversight of program; (3) much of the pastoral care; (4) music; (5) building, nurturing, supporting, and enlisting replacements for that network of volunteers; and (6) most of the teaching ministry. If the senior minister insists, "I can do this and maybe even three or four of those and all we need is a couple of people to pick up what I don't have time to do," it clearly is time to choose one of two forks in the road. Either forget about becoming a full-service church or replace that senior minister!

One of the most clear-cut reasons why so many large congregations plateau at between six and seven hundred in worship is because the senior minister is unable or unwilling to delegate responsibilities.

If the goal is to move past seven hundred at worship, the senior minister probably will have to be comfortable delegating to other staff members the primary responsibility for part or all of these six responsibilities: (1) community ministries, (2) administration, (3) oversight of program and the group life, (4) pastoral care, (5) building and caring for that huge network of volunteers, and (6) the enlistment and assimilation of new members.

If the goal is to move past twelve hundred at worship, the senior minister probably will have to delegate the primary responsibility for all six plus share part of the worship and preaching load.

If the goal is to move beyond an average attendance of eighteen hundred at worship, the senior minister probably will have to concentrate largely on three concerns: (1) enriching and expanding corporate worship with the help of other staff, (2) conceptualizing and articulating the vision of what the Lord is calling this parish to be and to do tomorrow and working to transform that vision into reality, and (3) identifying and treating minor symptoms of impending problems before they can become disasters. The third often calls for a listening ear, a warm heart, an open mind, a keen eye for detail, and expertise as a diagnostician in distinguishing between symptoms and problems.

In summary, this approach to staffing begins with an affirmation of the gifts and skills of the senior minister and a determination to make the best use of those gifts and skills by carefully staffing what the senior minister will not do. Most existing congregations that want to become full-service churches have only three alternatives: (1) staff to complement and supplement the gifts and skills of the current senior minister, (2) decide to be a Sunday morning church, or (3) decide to replace the present senior minister.

This affirmation of the central role of the senior minister troubles many people. It often arouses dissent from those who believe every pastor should be an enabler or facilitator, not an initiating leader. It disturbs those who contend that "the laity should run the church." (See chapter 5.) It violates the value systems of those who prefer that the senior minister be perceived simply as one member of a program staff team. It worries those who are concerned about creating a "personality cult." It violates the teachings of many seminary professors and denominational officials. It is in conflict with the polity of several denominations. (The big exceptions are the Roman Catholic Church, the Anglican Church, the Episcopal Church, and most Methodist denominations.) It often evokes considerable hostility from volunteer leaders who see their long-held power being eroded by the arrival of a new senior minister who is an initiating and venturesome leader.

This affirmation of the central role of the senior pastor is completely compatible with the culture of the large black churches in urban America, with the style of congregational life in the relatively new, large, and rapidly growing nondenominational full-service Anglo churches still served by the founding pastor, with many of the large Anglo Sunday morning churches of the 1950s served by a long-tenured senior minister, and with the style of ministerial leadership found in most of the very largest congregations affiliated with any of the mainline Anglo denominations *if that church is reaching large numbers of adults born after 1955.*

Seven Other Key Roles

After thirty-two years of working with churches of all sizes from scores of different religious traditions, I am completely convinced that the key variable in the creation and the continued functioning of the seven-day-a-week church is the senior minister. It is equally clear that one pastor cannot accomplish this without help. While they differ in age, personality, gifts, gender, responsibilities, and background, seven other roles usually can be identified in the healthy, effective, vital, growing, and attractive seven-day-a-week churches. In some congregations one role is shared, either concurrently or sequentially, by two or more individuals. In others, one individual has accepted and completely filled one role for years and years. Three or four usually are highly visible to nearly everyone. Four, and sometimes as many as six, of these roles are filled by paid staff, but volunteers often fill the first three.

Who Will Tell the Truth?

The larger the size of the congregation and/or the more rapid the pace of numerical growth and/or the more attractive it is to people who have not been actively involved in the life of any worshiping community for years and/or the more extensive the total ministry and program, the larger the proportion of people who depart every year. The vast majority leave silently, many are never missed, and only rarely do the leaders discover the real reasons behind these departures. Many leave because their personal spiritual pilgrimage leads them to another religious community. A few go because they are convinced their presence is no longer needed, and they go where they believe they will be needed. Others eventually conclude that this really is not the right church for them after all. Some depart because of their dissatisfaction with current policies and practices.

The one characteristic they share is that most do not articulate their complaints to the staff. The larger the flood of new people coming in, the easier it is to ignore the exodus. One consequence of this combination of size, high turnover, fast-paced programming, tight schedules, excitement, continued growth, and focus on tomorrow is that the senior minister may never hear the whole truth.

Thus the rarest, the most valuable, and the most difficult to fill of these seven roles is the person who will speak the truth to the senior minister in a manner that causes those words to be heard and digested. This can be a powerful force in the process of self-correction. Not all senior ministers want to hear the truth, and at least a few cannot accept it. Their tendency is to want to silence or discredit the bearer of what they interpret, not as the truth, but rather as bad news. For those who not only can hear, but also are willing to benefit from hearing the truth, the bearer of the truth may be perceived as the most valuable player on the team.

The older the senior minister, the longer the seniority over both paid staff and volunteer leaders, the higher the level of competence, and the greater the authority that is concentrated in that office, the more difficult it is for ordinary human beings to speak the truth to that senior minister. It is far easier to depart silently.

Who accepts this role and the obligations that go with it? It may be the senior minister's spouse, that pastor's secretary, an adult son or daughter, a brother or sister, a close friend from among the volunteer leaders, perhaps an older program staff member, a member of the choir, a fellow pastor, or, rarely, a denominational leader. If the senior minister sincerely wants that role to be filled, this ranks at the top of these seven!

Who Is the Pastor's Pastor?

While many bishops and holders of the equivalent position in other denominations often identify themselves as "a pastor to pastors," this reflects a problem in role definition. Only the person being ministered to can identify who is his or her pastor. Rarely do senior ministers of very large churches turn to a denominational official to be their pastor. Who fills the role of pastor to the senior minister of the very large church?

The deacons? The board of elders? A fellow staff member? A neighboring minister? A former seminary professor? A close friend from within that parish? Another senior pastor?

One response to that question is the group of five to seven volunteer leaders who meet with the senior minister every Tuesday for an hour or two of Bible study, prayer, mutual support, shared love, and conversation.

Another response is "Beats me!"

Another response is "My spouse."

Another response is "A friend who has the cabin next to ours at the lake."

Another is "A group of senior ministers from all across the country whom I meet with for three days twice a year."

Another is the president or moderator of that congregation.

Too often the answer is "No one."

The Ally and Legitimizer

The third critical role often filled by one or more volunteer leaders is the individual who helps to legitimize the vision of the pastor, who serves as the number-one ally of the senior minister, and who knows how to build support for that dream. Who is this person? Frequently these persons are identified by other members in sentences such as what follows.

"If Austin favors that, it must be okay, so you can count on my support."

"If Maggie will agree to chair the committee, I'll serve on it."

"If Terry suggested we do it, I say let's do it!"

"If that's what Pat recommends, I think we should do it."

"Tell me how Chris feels about it, and I'll tell you whether it's worth trying."

"If Kelly wants it, let's do it!"

In the best of the seven-day-a-week churches every organization, class, choir, group, circle, committee, task force, and new program includes at least one member who is a committed ally of the senior minister, who is a respected legitimizer of this week's dream that may turn into next month's newest ministry, and who helps to resell the vision of a new tomorrow.

Who Cares for Me?

The atmosphere in some large congregations is cluttered with a distracting mixture of petty complaints, endless griping, irrelevant criticisms, quiet grumbling, and continuous fault-finding. In many others the atmosphere is almost completely free of that kind of internal verbal pollution. Why the difference? Is one group of people more spiritual or more forgiving or more Christian than the other? Or does polity or denominational affiliation account for the difference? Or is this a reflection of staff harmony or the absence of staff harmony?

The second best explanation probably reflects the difference between growing institutions and those that are shrinking in size. Organizations, including churches and denominations, that are experiencing quantitative growth and also are reaching younger generations of people often display a greater tolerance for diversity, less interest in doing yesterday over again, and easier acceptance of new ideas. They usually find it easier to implement new goals. They also move at a faster pace than the organizations that are growing older and smaller. Thus that polluted atmosphere filled with petty bickering and pointless griping often is a product of the process of growing older and smaller.

The third best explanation is that this is a product of inadequate internal communication.

A more common explanation is that the complaining, griping, backbiting, grumbling, and bickering are symptoms of a deeper and more serious problem. Frequently that is the absence of an adequate level of pastoral care.

In other words, staffing the large church to provide an adequate level of pastoral care of the members not only provides certain obvious direct benefits, but it also produces significant fringe benefits!

In smaller congregations this responsibility normally falls on the pastor. Larger churches often bring on staff a semi-retired, loving, mature, person-centered (as contrasted with task-oriented), caring, hardworking, and highly committed minister to carry one part of that load while the other staff members share the rest of the responsibility for pastoral care.

The very large churches usually choose from among one of three alternative patterns. One is to add a full-time specialist in pastoral care and expect that person to do most of it. The second is to seek a staff person who will cause it to happen partly by doing it, but largely by building and overseeing a highly redundant system that is designed to provide at least an adequate level of pastoral care for every person in that congregation. One component may be a training program for lay volunteers to enable them to carry part of the responsibility.[2] A second component is to enable every class, group, choir, organization, circle, commission, task force, and cell to accept at least part of the responsibility for the care of the people in that sub-unit of the congregation. A third component is to clarify the responsibility of every staff person for providing one slice of the total ministry of pastoral care. A fourth is to station one staff member at every exit from the sanctuary to greet and/or hug and/or inquire "How are you?" and/or shake the hand and/or listen attentively for a few seconds to those who leave the worship experience through that exit. A fifth is to clarify the assignments of the staff so that every Sunday morning one or two program staffers roam the halls, greet early arrivals, and watch for signals. A sixth is to build and maintain a sensitive internal communication system so that "the office" does receive the messages being sent. A seventh is to organize a small corps of dedicated volunteer greeters who accept this as their number-one volunteer assignment. This is the opposite of the "rotating greeter" system. This system means that the same greeter will be in the same place Sunday after Sunday *and will be listening attentively*. This is a critical component of that sensitive internal communication system and means messages must be received and passed on to the appropriate person.

For churches seeking to reach and serve families with young children, the nursery often is a source of important messages on needs. For churches serving people born before 1970, the adult Sunday school classes and the circles in the women's organization can be valuable sources of messages.

A third approach to pastoral care combines the first two. The trained staff specialist in pastoral care works with another staff member. The specialist concentrates on providing direct services (hospital calls, counseling, etc.) while the second person builds and oversees that larger network.

The basic generalization is that the older the people and/or the more rapid the turnover rate in the membership and/or the greater the degree of diversity in the clientele being served and/or the longer the congregation has been in existence, the greater the need for adequate staffing of this ministry of pastoral care.

Functional or Motivational?

These differing approaches to pastoral care also illustrate a fundamental distinction in staffing. As was emphasized earlier, the most widely followed philosophy is to hire staff members to do specific tasks. A far less common, but far more difficult, philosophy calls for staff members to identify, enlist, train, motivate, place, and support volunteers in both ministry and administration.

This concept has been widely discussed and vigorously advocated for decades, especially by pastors in smaller congregations. It usually is identified by such labels as facilitator, enabler, servant leadership, or empowerment of the laity. The widespread implementation of that philosophy of ministerial leadership in small congregations has been limited by several factors. Among these are (1) most small congregations want a minister who is a doer, not a facilitator; (2) this role requires an exceptionally high level of competence, including the ability to transform the expectations of the members; (3) it normally requires a minimum of a fifteen-year pastorate to install and institutionalize this style of ministerial leadership; (4) it is in conflict with the policy and culture of several religious traditions; (5) it works best when the congregation includes a minimum of three exceptionally competent potential volunteer leaders and workers who are not actively involved in the work of standing ministries or in the teaching ministry and thus are free to staff new expressions of ministry; and (6) it is compatible with a budget in which no more than 40 percent of total expenditures are allocated to staff compensation, thus leaving substantial amounts for funding new ministries, programs, and expressions of outreach.

An increasing number of large seven-day-a-week program churches have chosen the motivational route in building their staff. First of all, of course, this requires a long-tenured senior minister who unreservedly believes in this philosophy. Second, it requires the unqualified support of the volunteers who have a voice in selecting staff. Third, it usually means training or retraining new staff members in this style of ministry. Those who do not work effectively in this role have a short tenure. Fourth, it means that every effort must be made to extend the tenure of those staff members who are effective motivators. Fifth, and this is critical, it requires building and reinforcing a congregational culture that is compatible with and supportive of this style of staff leadership.

One example of the implementation of the motivational approach to staffing may be in how the responsibilities for the pastoral care of the members are implemented. A second may be in staffing the ministry of music.

The Beat of a Different Drummer

One traditional view of music in the churches is to see it as enriching corporate worship. Another is to see it as an activity with the carol choir for young children, a handbell group for mature adults, and a youth choir for one group of teenagers. A third perspective recognizes and affirms the power of music as a central organizing principle for very large groups of people.

By definition, the program church should see music as all of these, but more specifically as a crucial component of the total ministry. This can be illustrated in the search for staff. The congregation averaging two hundred at worship often seeks a part-time choir director who can organize and direct a high-quality chancel choir. If that individual also can and will organize an attractive youth choir, that is a fringe benefit.

The congregation averaging four hundred at worship often seeks a staff person who can organize and direct an excellent chancel choir and also will produce three to seven other music groups (two children's choirs, a brass group, a youth choir, a handbell group, and a flute choir) that will "perform" during worship. One way to increase the frequency of attendance among the members is to schedule at least three music groups in each worship service.

The full-service or program church usually will have a broader range of goals in building and staffing the ministry of music. These may include (1) a minimum of three music groups in every Sunday morning worship experience, (2) a superb chancel choir that challenges participants to sing better than they know how to sing, (3) a spectacular event built around music every Advent that attracts a combined attendance of three thousand to thirty thousand at the five to seven times it is presented in December, (4) a music program that provides dozens of attractive entry points to future members of this congregation, (5) an orchestra or band, (6) a religious drama offered every spring to the general public, (7) three or four points for continuing participation by teenagers, (8) instruction in both vocal and instrumental music, (9) enrichment for the Sunday school, (10) a recognition of the power of enthusiastic congregational singing, (11) music encounter experiences with instrumental music for young children, (12) the only men and boys choir in that county or at least a men's chorus, (13) several components of that larger system for the assimilation of new members into the congregation, (14) four to seven specialized instrumental groups, including a brass group and a string group, (15) a "fun choir" for those who want to sing in the choir at the first service on Sunday morning, but the only time acceptable to all for rehearsal is at eleven o'clock Sunday morning, and (16) most important of all, a recognition that music can be one of the most divisive issues in a highly pluralistic congregation.

Thus when the time comes to staff the ministry of music, the beginning point may be to find someone to head it who (1) will insist "we expand this list from sixteen to at least twenty components," (2) is comfortable with ambiguity and complexity, (3) enjoys working with both volunteers and paid music staff rather than wanting to do it all, (4) enthusiastically and sincerely affirms the value of offering people a range of choices in music, (5) recognizes the need to design one worship service around one approach to music while turning to a radically different form of music for another service, and (6) is comfortable with a program goal that places participation above perfection in the list of priorities, while another goal places perfection ahead of participation.[3]

In other words, seek someone who can act on the assumption that the seven-day-a-week church has competing drummers, each with a different beat and each attracting a different following, and sincerely affirm that it is good. One alternative is to have several part-time specialists in music, each with a precisely defined responsibility and all working under the oversight of the program director.

The Program Director

One of the newest and fastest growing vocations in American Protestantism is the position of program director. In scores of very large congregations the three most valuable players on the staff team are the program director, the secretary to the senior pastor, and the senior pastor. The rank order in terms of value of those three varies from church to church.

A common pattern has been for the Sunday morning church to expand the position of Director of Christian Education to Program Director as part of a larger strategy to become a seven-day-a-week church. That has provided one source of program directors. Others are ordained ministers who prefer this specialized vocation to serving as a generalist. A few are pre-retirement pastors. A significant and growing source consists of mothers who have discovered they no longer are needed on a full-time basis in the home and build on earlier experiences plus their skills as mothers plus that foundation as an active volunteer in the church to move into this role. An increasing number are women who move from similar responsibilities in public or private employment into the church as program directors.

The big variable is the degree to which the senior minister delegates oversight of the program to this person. That means it is impossible to write a universal job description. The expectations must be shaped to fit that particular set of local circumstances.

The best program directors display at least a half-dozen of these characteristics: (1) creativity, (2) a high level of productivity, (3) deep sensitivity to other people, (4) enthusiasm, (5) high moral character, (6) a strong future orientation, (7) an eagerness to tackle the unknown, (8) competence in overseeing the work of both volunteers and paid staff, (9) a far above average ability to enlist volunteers and to work with other people, and (10) unreserved loyalty toward the senior pastor. (This tends to be more common among lay program directors than among the clergy.)

The Executive Pastor

Two of the pieces of baggage that go with the role of the large program church are (1) an increase in complexity and (2) an increase in administrative responsibilities.

One consequence is that many large churches talk about moving into that role, but never do because those price tags are too high. Another is the frustration of the overworked senior pastor who refuses to delegate responsibility. A third is the sharp drop in attendance and the cutback in programming when the new senior minister is overwhelmed by that combination of administrative responsibilities and complexity. In other churches the admonition is "If we all would work a little harder," or "If we all would cooperate more fully," the complexity and administrative burden would disappear.

A more sophisticated response is to create and fill the position of executive pastor. Typically, this is a response to the span-of-control issue. When the number of full-time program staff members (or the equivalent in full-time and part-time staff) exceeds six or seven, the time has arrived to create this position *and to assign the appropriate responsibilities to the person who fills that role.*

Executive pastors come from a variety of backgrounds. A majority are ordained ministers. Many of the best have been promoted from lay administrative assistant to the senior minister. Others come from public or private employment or from the military service.

The number-one quality needed in an effective executive pastor is loyalty to the senior minister. That is followed by (1) an unreserved Christian commitment, (2) character, (3) an understanding of the crucial importance of keeping certain bits of information confidential, (4) administrative skills, (5) ability to oversee a staff, (6) competence in church finances, (7) compatibility with the role and style of ministry of that parish, (8) productivity, (9) an understanding of two-way accountability, (10) an ability to implement goals, (11) earned credibility, and (12) a strong, but not necessarily big, ego.

Wesley E. Kiel, the executive minister in a large Reformed congregation in Holland, Michigan, undertook an extensive study of executive pastors. Using the Myers-Briggs Type Indicator, he found that the two most common personality types among the people he interviewed and tested were ENTJ and ESTJ with ISTJ third. (In the system, *T* represents thinking, as contrasted with *F* for feeling; *J* represents judging, as contrasted with *P* for perceiving; *E* represents extroversion, as contrasted with *I* for introversion; and *S* represents sensing, as contrasted with *N* for intuition.[4])

Kiel also speculates that senior pastors who are NF (intuitive-feeling) probably will get along best with the ENTJ or the ESTJ executive pastor because (1) these senior pastors are strong in building relationships with people, (2) their personality type complements the ENTJ or ESTJ executive pastor, (3) the extroverted (E) executive pastor will be comfortable working with that relational senior minister, (4) senior ministers, by definition of that role, will see and affirm the value of staff with complementing gifts and personalities, and (5) both will display a strong future orientation.

In simple terms, the senior minister articulates and repeatedly resells the vision that determines the direction this congregation is headed,[5] the program director helps to create and oversee the program that is compatible with and supportive of that role and direction, while the executive pastor makes sure the institution is functioning effectively, happily, and with the minimum number of malfunctions.

In addition to these essential members of the staff team for the large and rapidly growing program church, several other people will be necessary. Their exact titles and responsibilities vary tremendously, depending on the qualifications of other staff members, the program priorities, the size of the congregation, and the style or focus of ministry. Among the more valuable are (1) the secretary to the senior pastor; (2) the person responsible for creating, nurturing, supporting, and enlisting replacements for that huge network of volunteers; (3) the director of the Early Childhood Development Center and/or the principal of the Christian Day School; (4) the receptionist who excels on the telephone and can respond to at least 70 percent of all telephone calls for information; and (5) the person responsible for building and overseeing that growing package of ministries with families that include young children.

Independent Entrepreneurs or Staff Team?

One of the biggest forks in the road in staffing the full-service congregation often reflects the personality, preferences, and priorities of the senior minister. One highly productive alternative is to conceptualize the total program as a series of semi-autonomous empires. Each one of these empires is served by a staff member who is a visionary and motivational leader. Each program area has its own policy-making board of volunteers, many of whom have been enlisted by that staff member.

The director of the early childhood development center is a remarkably productive, enthusiastic, high energy, entrepreneurial, visionary, and creative empire builder who expects the size of the program to double in five years. The minister of music, with the backing of an exceptionally supportive music committee, is always (1) creating new music groups and (2) pleading for a larger budget. The program director has detailed plans for doubling the teaching ministry and tripling the number of special events, activities, mutual support groups, and new classes during the next few years. The minister of ministries with families that include teenagers is confident, given additional resources, that ministry could triple in size in five years. The minister of community ministries is frequently accused of "stealing" volunteers from other programs to staff

110

that rapidly growing bundle of outreach ministries. Many members are convinced that this is an extravagant approach to ministry.

The senior minister seeks entrepreneurial personalities who are motivational leaders for the program staff, enjoys watching the growing competition among them, laughs at the problems this creates for the executive pastor, helps to raise the money necessary to fund this giant circus, and adjourns program staff meetings with the admonition "Sic 'em!"

The governing board focuses on tomorrow, draws generous boundaries for what is acceptable here at this time, delegates most of the worrying to the executive pastor, the finance committee, the trustees, and the senior pastor, and laughs when accused of encouraging chaos. The finance committee concentrates on making sure receipts exceed expenditures.

A widely advocated and far more difficult to implement alternative is to conceptualize the total ministry of that congregation as one giant coherent package. All the components within that package are internally consistent with all other components. Each reinforces and undergirds every other component. Teamwork, not competition, is the key word in describing staff relationships. This is the model of choice of many program staff members in Sunday morning churches. The governing board, not the various program committees, formulates policies, determines priorities, and makes the final decisions on all matters of consequence. Coordination, efficiency, economy, simplicity, and teamwork are highly valued principles. The executive pastor is expected to be a manager, not a leader.[6] The overall coordination of staff rests with the senior minister. Considerable time in staff meetings is devoted to schedules and to minimizing competition and conflict. The finance committee sees that its primary responsibility is to keep expenditures below receipts and to encourage efficiency in the allocation of scarce resources.

This dream of creating a staff that functions as a team has much to commend it, but it is difficult to implement. Two experts on this subject have written that successful teams usually display these eight characteristics: (1) a clear and elevating goal that is internally consistent and accepted by every member of the team as the number-one goal; (2) a results- or performance-driven structure; (3) competent team members; (4) a high level of unified commitment; (5) a collaborative climate (or congregational culture or environment); (6) high expectations and standards of excellence; (7) external (from that team) support, encouragement, and recognition, and (8) principled leadership.[7] Many full-service churches are too diverse and too complicated to nurture those characteristics.

The nature of American Protestantism suggests that it may be easier to meet all eight of those standards or criteria for building a successful team in the smaller Sunday morning church than in the large and rapidly growing program church.

Who Staffs New Ministries?

A question that arises repeatedly in large program churches is over the staffing of new ministries. Most congregations pick one of two alternatives.

The more common is to bring a new person onto the payroll to staff that new ministry. This can be a highly productive approach when that new staff member is a longtime member who has been an active volunteer and who helped to initiate the creation of that new ministry. That usually means the new staffer is familiar with and supportive of the distinctive culture of that congregation, has earned the trust and confidence of both the paid staff and volunteer leaders, understands the purpose of this new ministry, and is supportive of the reasons for creating it. Sometimes this individual joins the staff on a part-time basis and subsequently becomes full-time. On other occasions this is seen as either a permanent full-time position or as a permanent part-time job.

In other churches the search is limited to non-members. That usually means the new staff member is confronted with four big assignments from day one. The obvious assignment is to turn the dream of a new ministry into reality. Sometimes the new staffer brings a different interpretation of that dream than is held by those who created it. In addition that new staffer must (1) discern and understand the distinctive culture of this parish, (2) earn the trust and confidence of other staff members and volunteer leaders, and (3) build a volunteer support group for that new ministry. That is a big assignment for a new staff member!

One alternative to adding a new person to the payroll to staff new ministries is winning more and more support. This is to reduce the work load of a long-tenured staff member who is freed to staff that new ministry. This may begin with staffing the committee of volunteers that creates the dream. This staff person already knows and is comfortable with the culture of the congregation; presumably has earned the respect, trust, and confidence of the rest of the staff plus the key volunteer leaders; knows where all the bodies are buried; has meaningful "ownership" in the proposal and understands the reasons behind it; and is familiar with the people who constitute most of the potential volunteer support group required to turn that dream into reality.

Instead of hiring someone to staff that new program, someone is added to the payroll to pick up the responsibilities vacated by the long-tenured staffer who is assigned to that new program. This means that the new program staffer comes on board to work on one or more ministries that already have their own volunteer support groups, have built up considerable momentum, and have completed that difficult "shakedown cruise." The learning curve already is moving up when the new staffer comes on the scene.

This alternative reduces the burden on the new staff person and also increases the chances that the new ministry will closely resemble the dream of those who pioneered it.

A completely different alternative has become available in recent years with the emergence of more and more teaching churches. This alternative often follows a four-part sequence. First, a task force or ad hoc study committee, sometimes at the initiative of a program staff member, identifies the need. Second, that group begins to conceptualize what that new ministry could look like in response to that need. Third, and this is the critical component of this sequence, that task force invites three program staff persons who are specializing in that particular ministry in three larger churches to come and spend a Saturday with that task force. These three outsiders constitute a panel and (a) describe each church's experiences in that specialized ministry, (b) respond to questions from members of the task force, (c) offer suggestions on staffing it, and (d) point out potential problems and pitfalls. Fourth, after that experience, the task force decides whether to recommend asking a current staff member to carry this responsibility or to seek a new staff member. Sometimes the members of the panel can suggest candidates for that position. Occasionally that panel is asked to interview persons who are perceived to be potential candidates for that staff position. This can be the best beginning point in creating and staffing a new ministry.

Some students of the American Protestant church scene will argue that this discussion overlooks a critical variable in staffing—the polity and the denominational system for congregational self-government. That is an important point, and it is especially influential in staffing smaller congregations. The larger the size of the congregation, however, and the more varied the weekday program, the more likely the actual system of governance will reflect, rather than direct, that staffing configuration. That statement explains the sequence for this and the next chapter.

CHAPTER FIVE

Who Runs That Big Church?

Befor moving here, my wife and I spent nearly fifteen years in a church that always tried to follow the Holy Scriptures in everything we did," explained a sixty-three-year-old man who had joined a very large program church several months earlier and subsequently had sought an interview with the senior minister. "That was an elder-run church, and we followed Paul's instructions in his letter to Titus in selecting elders. I was elected an elder when I was fifty-one, soon after our youngest child was baptized, and I continued to serve as an elder until my company transferred me here about a year ago. My wife and I visited several churches before we settled on this one. We were looking for a Christ-centered church that preaches the Bible, and you do that here. But I have two questions."

"Go ahead and ask them," gently urged the puzzled senior minister.

"The first is one that just came up the other day," continued this layman. "I heard that one of our elders has been married, divorced, and remarried. Is that true?"

"Yes, that is true," replied the senior pastor. "I don't know to whom you are referring, but we do have two elders who are divorced and remarried."

"That's hard to believe," challenged the layman. "In the first chapter of his letter to Titus, Paul states very clearly that an elder can be married only once. Now you tell me that you have two elders who are divorced and remarried."

"Yup," replied the senior minister. "What's your second question?"

"I don't know whether it really matters after what you just told me," declared this obviously disillusioned recent new member, "but several people have said that you really run this church and the elder board simply rubber stamps what you recommend. Is that true?"

"Not quite," replied the slightly puzzled senior minister, who was having his first face-to-face and one-on-one conversation with this new member. "I know some of our people believe I run this church and the board of elders simply acts as a rubber stamp, but that is not an accurate representation of reality. For all practical purposes this church is run by the staff, not by me alone, with the advice, consent, support, and help of our board of elders plus about a dozen committees. People may see me as a dictator, but this church is run by the staff and me, plus about a hundred volunteer board and committee members and several hundred volunteers in doing ministry."

This brief conversation could be used to illustrate any one of several different points. It is but one of a dozen arguments to support the new-member orientation class that includes thirty-two to forty-five weekly sessions. That long-term class is consistent with the self-identified role as a high commitment church. That approach to new-member orientation also can be a useful component of a larger strategy for the assimilation of new members. That long series of teaching opportunities also can enable prospective new members to understand the polity, the doctrinal stance, the history, the mission, the role, the traditions, and the culture of the congregation they are seeking to join. It minimizes subsequent surprises for new members and also reduces the volume of traffic out that infamous "back door" through which members depart for greener pastures.

This conversation also could introduce how one interprets Scripture in today's social context. In his first Epistle to Timothy, Paul writes: "Let no one be enrolled as a widow who is under sixty years of age . . . but refuse to enroll younger widows" (I Tim. 5:9-11). Literally hundreds of Protestant churches today have discovered that among their most valuable paid staff members are widowed women in their fifties. Should they have been encouraged to remarry rather than to join the program staff?

Obviously this conversation also could introduce a discussion on the qualifications required for anyone to serve as a volunteer leader in the church today. This layman had spent many years in a Church of Christ congregation that rigidly enforced all of Paul's standards for lay volunteers to become elders, including (a) gender, (b) no child in the home that had not been baptized by believer's baptism, and (c) marital status.

For the purposes of this discussion, however, this conversation introduces one of the most critical issues facing the very large Protestant church. What is the system of governance? Who really runs the very large church? Who should run it?

One beginning point for responding to that question is highly pragmatic. Are there any differences among the governance systems of the churches in American Protestantism? The answer is that there are many. Among the sources of those differences are local traditions; the personality, background, leadership style, experience, tenure, and ideological stance of the present senior pastor; age of the congregation; age of the volunteer leaders; denominational polity; racial or national heritage; the rate of numerical growth or decline; the financial base; the position on the theological spectrum; and size.

Seven Patterns of Governance

When size is used as the central variable in examining the system of governance of Protestant congregations on the North American continent, seven patterns appear repeatedly without regard to the denominational identity.

The most common by far can be seen in thousands of long-established small churches. In these congregations, most of which average fewer than forty-five at worship, a handful of volunteers "run the church." Frequently the majority of these volunteer policy makers are third- or fourth-generation members, and their most influential credentials often include a deep sense of loyalty to that congregation, long tenure, persistence, good bloodlines, and a comprehensive knowledge of the past and of local traditions. In most of these long-established small churches, the minister does not become an influential policy maker before year three or four of his or her tenure, and too many depart before the end of year four.

In several respects these small congregations resemble a family in culture, interpersonal relationships, decision making, openness to outsiders, and role of the minister. That, of course, is one reason why they are able to survive highly disruptive experiences. That also is one reason they find it difficult to assimilate strangers into the fellowship, including those who marry a family member.

The minister's influence begins to become more powerful when we examine congregations that (a) average more than forty-five at worship and/or (b) are new missions that average fewer than forty-five at worship and/or (c) report the tenure of the pastor exceeds that of a majority of today's adult members.

In these congegations, which typically average between 45 and 125 at worship, a second pattern of governance usually appears. Instead of relying on that cadre of volunteers, with the premium on willingness rather than office or position, structure becomes more prominent. The official governing board and the minister, usually in that order, have most of the authority to make policy decisions. Frequently, this authority is shared with two or three committees (finance, Christian education, trustees). The longer the tenure of the minister, and the greater the degree of seniority the pastor has over volunteers, the more influential the point of view of that pastor. With that one exception, these still tend to be ''lay run'' churches. As a general pattern, the greater the power of the volunteers who do not hold official leadership positions and/or the weaker the authority of the pastor, (a) the shorter the average tenure of each pastor in that passing parade of ministers and (b) the more likely that the average attendance at worship will not exceed one hundred.

In these small to middle-sized congregations, the board members, sometimes with substantial help from the pastor, do everything. They make policy, enlist volunteers, repair the roof, talk, call on people, usher, prepare and serve meals, talk, wash windows, pray, paint, teach, study, talk, write letters, attend conferences, talk, quarrel, raise money, glorify the past, and rarely delegate policy-making responsibilities.

A third pattern frequently can be seen among congregations averaging between approximately 120 and 240 at worship. The distribution of influence and power has changed. The pastor often is the number-one authority figure, the governing board is second, and a larger share of the power is deposited in committees. The more reluctant the pastor is to accept that authority figure role and/or the weaker the committee structure, the more likely that congregation is (a) shrinking in size and (b) moving toward 100 at worship rather than toward 250.

The most common qualification for this third pattern is that on questions that may require substantial departures from the status quo for implementation, a final veto often is vested in the congregation as a whole.

This often means that a proposal initiated by the pastor and supported by a majority of the governing board and by a majority on the appropriate standing committee will be vetoed at a congregational meeting, if that proposed course of action is part of a larger strategy to sharply increase the size of that congregation. This is less an issue of power and control than it is a struggle between advocates of planned change (a minority in most congregations) and supporters of the status quo (a majority in most congregations). (This issue will be discussed at greater length later in this chapter.)

A similar distribution of power, but different because of one or more variations, represents a fourth pattern. This pattern is most common in congregations averaging between 225 and 450 at worship. The first variation in this pattern is when the pastor holds a remarkably large amount of power. Rarely is that a product of the polity or the denominational label. Usually that accumulation of power in the pastor is a product of three or more of these sources: (1) skill, (2) knowledge, (3) racial or ethnic or national or religious subculture, (4) leadership ability, (5) initiative, (6) productivity, (7) competence as a preacher-teacher-administrator-worship leader-pastor, (8) tenure, (9) seniority, (10) age, (11) experience, or (12) personality.

Those qualities not only explain the greater power of that pastor, but they also often explain why that congregation is averaging 350 to 450 at worship rather than 175 to 225.

A second variation is that a substantial chunk of power and influence is held by other paid staff members, often including the church secretary, the choir director or minister of music, the full-time custodian, the associate minister, and others. This shift in power often is at the expense of the standing committees, who may become increasingly dependent on (subservient to?) the senior minister or the staff person who works with that standing committee.

A third variation in the governance of this group of congregations is the occasional ad hoc study committee and/or ad hoc action committee that exercises tremendous authority on a single issue. Examples include the authority exercised by the pulpit nominating committee charged with finding a new senior pastor, the ad hoc study committee that recommends a radical revision of the Sunday morning schedule, or the building planning committee that recommends a $2 million capital expenditure while the standing committee on finances debates the amount to budget for postage.[1]

A fifth pattern of congregational self-government often is found in congregations averaging between 450 and 1,200 at worship. In these churches the criteria for gaining and exercising power contrast sharply with the very small churches described earlier. In these smaller churches the chief sources of power usually are long tenure, a willingness to serve, good bloodlines, commitment, and election to a leadership office.

In the churches averaging 700 or more at worship, the major sources of power are information ("In the world of the blind, the one-eyed man is king."), competence, commitment, time, and specialized skills. This means those staff members who carry large quantities of information in their heads, who work at the job fifty to seventy hours a week, who possess specialized skills, who are highly committed, not only to Jesus Christ but also to the life, ministry, and future of that congregation, and who are reasonably competent acquire considerable power.

It is rare for more than one or two volunteers to be able and willing to invest the amount of time week after week to be that well informed. The best informed volunteers usually specialize in one narrow slice of the total ministry, but rarely possess the information about the total life of that congregation that is in the head of the senior minister.

This raises another distinction between the very small and tradition-bound church and the very large and ministry-driven congregation. In the former, knowledge of the past, including the past history of individual members, frequently is a significant source of power. Rarely is that as useful in the big program church as knowledge about contemporary reality and a commitment to the vision that will shape the future. While dozens of volunteers in the large church may possess huge quantities of knowledge about the past, when compared to most staff members, that usually is only a minor source of power.

Regardless of the ideological attractiveness of creating a lay-run church, that rarely is feasible in the very large program congregation. It simply is too difficult to enlist competent volunteers who can and will invest the necessary time week after week to become completely knowledgeable about all aspects of the program, life, and ministry of that seven-day-a-week church. Most find they must trust the data base that staff bring to the policy-making table.

One exception to that generalization is when power is shared among staff and volunteers working on various program, administrative, and ad hoc committees. This usually means that (a) the governing board comes in third behind staff and committees in the distribution of knowledge and power and that (b) the congregation functions as a loose federation of semi-autonomous fiefdoms. This is more likely to be acceptable if each fiefdom, regardless of whether it is "run" largely by an individual staff member or by three or four highly knowledgeable committee members, has its own independent income stream. This may be from designated giving, endowment funds, memorials, rents, user fees, or a combination of these. The most common example of this is the board of trustees who are responsible for the real estate with a limited accountability to the governing board. Other examples may be the missions committee, the hunger commission, or a social action task force.

The sixth pattern often appears in congregations averaging between 1,200 and 2,800 at worship. The three most influential holders of power are (1) the senior minister and staff, (2) a series of ad hoc committees, and (3) the governing board. In this pattern the role of the governing board may resemble what is described as a "professional board" in a subsequent section of this chapter. Sometimes, but not always, this pattern minimizes the power of standing committees in favor of placing greater authority in task forces, caucuses, ad hoc committees, and self-funding groups. The greater the authority of these ad hoc groups, the more likely other leaders will complain about "the absence of any clearly defined strategy or goals to govern the allocation of scarce resources" such as money, volunteers, and staff time.

Finally, in perhaps one-half of all Protestant congregations averaging over 2,700 at worship, a radically different system of governance prevails. For all practical purposes, these very large congregations are run by the staff and a half-dozen or fewer volunteer leaders. The governing board composed of lay volunteers does not exist. The focus is on ministry and quality, not on enabling volunteers to make policy. With the exception of that half-dozen or fewer volunteers, all volunteer time is allocated to doing ministry, not administration. One of the benefits of this is that the vast majority of volunteers gain their greatest satisfaction from doing ministry, not administration. Those volunteers who express a need for control and want to specialize in administration tend to avoid these churches.

This strong emphasis on quality and the pursuit of excellence shifts most of the policy-making control to staff. It also encourages volunteers to specialize in those areas of ministry where they can excel. Excellence, superior performance, creativity, productivity, a continuing and relevant response to the religious and personal needs of an ever-changing constituency, and faithfulness to the gospel are the top priorities in these ministry-driven churches. Rotation of volunteers in office, the search for a concensus, participatory democracy, giving every voice equal weight, perpetuating the status quo, reinforcing tradition, and making life easier for the pastor rank at the bottom of the list of values and goals in these churches.

Six Observations

The purpose of this discussion is not to suggest that one pattern of governance is superior to all others. The purpose is simply to provide a context for looking at the alternatives open to the very large program church. Before moving into that discussion, however, it may be useful to offer a half-dozen general observations about governance.

First, in the overwhelming majority of Protestant congregations in the United States, the leaders perceive their congregation to be smaller, when compared to all other churches, than it really is. The larger the size of the congregation, the larger the discrepancy between perception and reality. One product of that discrepancy is the temptation to project excessively modest goals for the future. A second is the predictable tendency to prefer a system of governance that is appropriate for a smaller congregation.

Second, the choice of an inappropriate system of congregational self-government often is one of the seven most formidable barriers to numerical growth. (The other six are (1) the absence of competent, creative, inspiring, and initiating ministerial leadership; (2) limited financial resources; (3) location and physical facilities; (4) a position on the theological spectrum that is attractive to very few church shoppers; (5) a large contingent of articulate and influential members who want to do yesterday over again, only better; and (6) placing institutional needs—renovate the building, balance the budget, support denominational institutions and programming, increase the compensation of the minister—rather than the religious and personal needs of people, at the top of the priority list).

Third, the larger the number of senior ministers who have served that congregation during the past three decades, the higher the probability the congregation is using a system of governance that is appropriate for a much smaller church.

Fourth, in many large congregations the argument is inaccurately defined when it is stated as "lay voice versus clergy domination." Recent years have brought a rapid increase in the number of lay program staff members in large churches. A better statement of the argument may be "volunteer versus the professionals." Since the professionals usually bring a greater quantity of contemporary knowledge to the decision-making table than the volunteers possess, and since most of the professionals are full-time and the volunteers are part-time, this means that in the long run the professionals will prevail.

In many churches the best way to define that debate is to say that it really is between two points of view. One would be more comfortable with a system of governance that divides the power among the governing board, the standing committees, and the pastor, preferably in that order. This is an appropriate distribution for stable congregations averaging between 45 and 120 at worship with a low degree of complexity. The other side of that argument perceives this to be a large, complex, and rapidly changing congregation that requires a more centralized system for decision-making. In a sense, the debate is between those who prefer simplicity, a slower pace of congregational life, and stability versus those who accept complexity and a faster pace as the predictable pricetags of being a seven-day-a-week church.

A fifth observation is that many large and growing program churches are experiencing great frustration because they rely on a counterproductive system for making important policy decisions that have long-range consequences. One reason may be historical and traces back to the nineteenth century, when few congregations included more than two hundred members. A second reason may be the denominational polity or other local traditions designed to fit a smaller and less complex situation. A third is the heritage of "participatory democracy" from the 1960s.[2] A fourth factor is the genuine and sincere desire to offer every member an equal voice in decision making. This point of view holds that the vote of the member who attends corporate worship once every two years and contributes $10 annually should carry as much weight as the vote of the exceptionally well-informed member who rarely misses corporate worship, contributes $10,000 annually, and devotes an average of fifteen hours a week to that church.

This system of governance requires that every proposal for change be submitted for approval at a congregational meeting at which each member will have one vote. This includes the proposed budget for next year, the recommendation to create a new program staff position, the possibility of constructing an addition to the building, or a revision of the Sunday morning schedule.

To be effective this system of congregational government in the 1,500-member church requires that sufficient time be taken to enable every member to be equally well informed about the decisions and to attend that meeting. That often is time consuming, if not impossible.

Because it usually is easier to mobilize those who are opposed to change to come out to the congregational meeting than it is to motivate those who are happy with how things are going, this system really is biased against change.[3]

Another expression of counterproductive behavior in governance that is widely used to immobilize the decision-making processes of a large church has three components. The first is a widely respected staff specialist with a high degree of competence in one area of ministry. The second is the assumption that this competence in one area of congregational life creates an equal level of competence in all areas of the life and ministry of that parish. The third is the successful demand by supporters of that staff member that a co-pastorate be created, giving that staff member authority equal to the authority of the senior minister, but that responsibility for the consequences of those decisions be borne solely by the senior minister.

This strategy also has three common fringe consequences. The most obvious is to minimize the chances of numerical growth. A second is to place means-to-an-end issues at the top of the agenda above doing ministry. This is an effective means of attracting the participation of those who are deeply interested in such issues and of repelling the participation of those who prefer to focus on doing ministry. Third, it may be a means of hastening the premature departure of an effective senior minister.

A summary statement of this fifth observation explains the inclusion of this chapter in this book. The larger the congregation and/or the faster the rate of numerical growth and/or the more extensive the weekday program and/or the greater the diversity among the people being served, the more likely that congregation will utilize a system of governance that is incompatible with the size, role, and complexity of that church. Excessively simplistic approaches to complex issues often produce counterproductive results.

The final observation concerns confusion about when it is appropriate to require a unanimous vote of approval by representatives of the people before adopting any motion that involves change.

The requirement of a unanimous vote has much to commend it when it is adopted by an ad hoc committee. It often is followed by the pastoral nominating committee seeking a new pastor, by the building planning committee that is charged with planning for a new buiding, by the site committee that is looking for the location to which the meeting place can be relocated, by the ad hoc committee seeking a stewardship consultant to guide a capital funds appeal, and by the committee that is charged with engaging a parish consultant.

It often is worth the extra time required to secure that unanimous approval of a specific recommendation or decision. Usually these ad hoc committees bring a high degree of homogeneity in the membership[4] to their deliberations, and they also focus on a single issue.

By contrast, the governing board of a congregation often is designed to be a far more heterogeneous collection of people representing a huge variety of interests, opinions, values, generations, priorities, and points of view. In addition, instead of concentrating on a single issue, the governing board normally has to make decisions on many different issues, questions, and policies.

Requiring a unanimous vote on every decision by the governing board often produces at least four results. First, a minority of one is given more power than the majority possesses. Second, it often slows the pace of decision making. Third, it usually means tradition, precedents, and local customs outweigh the religious needs of people when proposals for new ministries are introduced. Finally, it can be an effective means of reducing the number of future new members.

Seven Alternatives

"In the next few minutes, I want to bring two items to your attention," explained the chairperson of the finance committee at Central Church. "The first is that we now expect a shortfall in our financial affairs of approximately $75,000 by the end of the year. The budget that was approved at our annual meeting last January called for expenditures of $817,000 and was based on anticipated receipts of $825,000. It now appears, with less than five weeks to go, that our expenditures will be $812,000, or approximately $5,000 below budget, but our receipts are estimated to total only $737,000—and that assumes our receipts this December will at least match those of last December.

"The second issue you need to be aware of is that your finance committee projected expenditures of $860,900 for next year, an increase of approximately 6 percent," continued this lay leader, who had been asked to give a brief stewardship report at each of the two worship services on that last Sunday morning in November. "We have completed our stewardship program, and, on the basis of your pledges and estimates of giving for next year plus the adjustments we can make based on past experiences, our projection is that our receipts will be approximately $735,000, or about $125,000 short of our projected needs. Unless you folks find it possible to increase your giving next year over what your advance estimates suggest it will be, your finance committee will have to make substantial reductions in the proposed budget for next year."

After a couple of minutes of elaborating on these points, this lay leader stepped down out of the chancel and returned to a front pew in the crowded sanctuary as the associate pastor sought to recreate a climate supportive for the corporate worship of a loving, generous, and forgiving God.

Ten days earlier and a couple of hundred miles away at the much larger Trinity Church, five volunteers were meeting with three full-time staff members. One was the Reverend Doctor Lewis Pennock, the senior minister of this huge program church that averaged 1,700 at worship. A second was Terry Dixon, the thirty-eight-year-old executive pastor. The third was Violet Bryan, now in her twenty-third year on the staff of Trinity Church.

After opening the meeting with prayer, the Reverend Lewis Pennock addressed the five volunteer leaders: "As I explained when I asked you to come to this special meeting tonight, it now appears that our cash flow squeeze will be more serious than we anticipated last January. Last year, member giving totaled a shade over $2 million, about $85,000 more than our expenditures. At our annual meeting in January, we adopted a budget of $2.4 million for this year, recognizing that represented a 20 percent increase. It now appears that our receipts for the year will be a shade over $2.1 million. Violet estimates our shortfall will be about a quarter of a million dollars. Terry has studied this and would like to get your reactions to several alternatives."

"It seems to me we have four choices," explained the executive pastor. "In order to meet our cash flow needs, we've postponed a few expenditures, and we've borrowed $200,000 from internal reserves. Thus one alternative is to carry a deficit of perhaps $275,000 into the new year. A second is to cut back on our mission commitments. As you may recall, that $2.4 million includes over $600,000 for missions. We've paid out about two-thirds of that so far, but we could cover the cash flow problem by reducing our mission giving by $100,000 this year and by $175,000 for next year."

"Oh, we can't do that!" interrupted Steve Wilcox, who chaired the missions commission. "That would mean breaking faith not only with our people, but more important, with the people we have committed to help through these mission projects. That simply is an unacceptable alternative!"

The other four volunteer leaders nodded in unmistakable agreement with Steve.

"A third alternative is to postpone the remodeling of the educational wing we have scheduled for next spring," continued Terry. "That is estimated at $335,000. Postponing that would offset the anticipated deficit. The fourth alternative would be to go to our people, explain our problem, and ask for $275,000 in additional contributions. I've drafted a copy of two letters I'm suggesting we send to our people."

While passing out copies of the two proposed letters, Terry continued, "I am convinced that if we explain the situation, our people will respond. What do you think?"

The first draft Terry shared with the other seven people at that Thursday evening meeting explained the reasons behind the impending deficit, made a plea for cooperation to enable Trinity Church to finish the year with all bills paid and no deficit, and advised that a second letter would soon follow. The draft of the second letter summarized the need and suggested the $275,000 deficit could be met by one contribution of $10,000, five of $5,000 each, twenty of $1,500 each, one hundred of $1,000 each, one hundred of $500 each, five hundred of $100 each, and $10,000 in smaller contributions.

After forty minutes of discussion, it was agreed to send out the two letters a week apart. The only significant revisions were to add a sentence pointing out the increasd flexibility that accompanies ending a fiscal year with a surplus rather than a deficit, to affirm that all mission commitments must be paid in full, and to raise the target by $25,000 to an even $300,000 to increase the probability of finishing the year with a modest surplus. It was agreed that the senior minister and three of these volunteer leaders would sign the first letter while Terry, Violet, and the other two members of this ad hoc committee would sign the second letter.

The bulletin for the last Sunday in December carried a box thanking the people for their generous response and reporting that a total of $303,741 had been received in response to this special appeal.

Who Initiates?

This is not a lesson in how to eliminate a projected deficit. That is not the point of this chapter. While that brief speech by the chairperson of the finance committee at Central Church stands out as an example of how to discourage first-time visitors from returning, that is not the point. Likewise, the proposal at Central Church to make "substantial reductions" in the proposed budget for the coming year could be cited as an effective tactic for keeping a large congregation from growing into a megachurch—that is not the point.

It could be argued that these two responses to an impending deficit illustrate a critical distinction between most congregations and the very large churches. The natural tendency in most churches is for the leaders to react to circumstances. By contrast, the leaders in very large churches are far more willing to take a proactive stance, but that is not the central point of this pair of illustrations.

The crucial point is governance. Where is the responsibility for taking the initiative lodged? In standing committees, as at Central Church in this example? In the governing board? In the staff, as at Trinity Church in this illustration? Should the staff point out problems and wait for the volunteer leaders to respond? Or should staff wait for volunteer leaders to identify the problem and suggest a course of action? One side of this debate was articulated by John Stuart Mill in the middle of the nineteenth century. In his theory of representative government, *On Liberty and Considerations on Representative Government,* Mill distinguished between the role of people's representatives and the civil servants hired by government. The former should make policy.[5] The latter should administer but not initiate. For the first several decades of the twentieth century, this also was the textbook model for the relationship of the city manager to the elected city council members. This model of placing control of policy formulation in the hands of elected volunteer leaders has been incorporated into the congregational polity of American Protestantism. (By contrast, the polity of the Roman Catholic Church, Episcopal and Anglican parishes, The United Methodist Church, and, to a lesser degree, the Presbyterian churches, grants far greater authority to initiate to the pastor.)

The other side of this debate is argued by those who contend that the vast increase in the size and complexity of large modern institutions requires stronger executive leadership. The need is for strong centralized full-time professional leaders who can respond wisely, vigorously, consistently, and continuously with the growing number of problems that arise daily.[6] This is the argument made on behalf of a strong principal in the large high school; for a powerful President of the United States; for a governor who is willing to be an influential, creative, forceful, and initiating leader; for the chancellor of the huge state university who is perceived as a dictator by many of the faculty; for the farsighted chief executive officer of a profit-making corporation; and for the aggressive mayor of a rapidly growing city. This was an influential factor behind the change in the title of the head of staff of a large public library system from chief librarian to library director.

Is it reasonable to expect that the volunteer members of the local school board or the volunteer board members of the municipal hospital or the volunteer board members of the three thousand-member congregation can and will invest the time week after week that is required to be an informed policymaker? That may be a realistic goal for the board governing the one-room country school in 1933 or the seventy-member rural church or the local public library with only one paid staff member. It may even have been an appropriate system of governance for the private church-related college with an enrollment of three hundred students in 1935.

This discussion raises the first of three questions that must be answered as the large program church designs a system of governance. Who is charged with the responsibility for initiating leadership? At Central Church it clearly was the person chairing the finance committee. At

Trinity Church it was the senior minister and staff. In middle-sized congregations it may be the governing board. In small churches it may be any volunteer willing to take the initiative.

The second question is Who is expected to react to that initiative? At Central Church it appeared to be those who came on that particular Sunday morning in November. At Trinity Church it clearly was a special ad hoc committee of knowledgeable, responsible, and respected leaders called together by the senior minister.

The third question is Who has the authority to act? At Central Church it appears that it is the finance committee. At Trinity Church it clearly is that ad hoc committee.

When internally consistent and coherent answers have been given to those three questions, it will be easy to begin the process of designing a system of governance. That leads into the subject of alternatives.

The best alternative is to custom tailor a system of governance that is compatible with and supportive of (1) the role as a large seven-day-a-week program church; (2) continued numerical growth; (3) the gifts, skills, expertise, personality, and preferences of the senior minister; (4) building and keeping a creative, venturesome, energetic, productive, and committed program staff; (5) a style of congregational life that makes ministry, not administration, the top priority; (6) the place at which this congregation is located on the theological spectrum; and (7) the local priorities in ministry. (For example, if missions is to be given a high priority, the missions committee should be a powerful force in decision making.)

The easiest, and often the most counterproductive, alternative is to adopt the system of governance designed by that denomination. The reason this may not be advisable is that most denominational systems for congregational self-government have been designed (1) to fit the middle-sized church, (2) on the assumption that "one size fits all," (3) to simplify life for pastors and volunteer leaders as they move from one congregation to another, (4) to provide links between denominational agencies and congregational committees, and (5) to give the congregation as a whole a veto over any proposal for change. In a few traditions the polity has been designed on the assumption that the pastor should be perceived as an employee of the governing board. This is at the other end of the spectrum from the tradition that assumes the current pastor was called by God to serve this congregation and, therefore, speaks with authority given by God.

A third, and widely followed, system of governance places the governing board at the center of the universe with all committees, both standing and ad hoc, as well as all paid staff members ultimately accountable to that governing board. This is a practical system in smaller, stable congregations where the governing board is able and willing to accept that initiating role described earlier. This usually is a comfortable alternative for the Sunday morning church that is happy to grow older and smaller and is served by a pastor who prefers to be an "enabler" or a "facilitator" rather than accept the role of an initiating leader.

A fourth alternative is to place most of the responsibility for initiative in (1) the senior pastor and staff, (2) standing committees, and (3) special ad hoc study committees.

This removes most of the responsibility for initiating changes from the governing board and defines its role very clearly. This alternative also is attractive to a growing number of church members because it is compatible with their past experiences. Literally thousands of lay leaders come to serve on the governing board of a Protestant church after years of experience on the board of some other non-profit organization or voluntary association. They come with a comparatively high level of experience, sophistication, and skill as board members.[7] Sometimes they are described as "professional" board members. A growing proportion of these volunteers are adult females.

For many, but not all, previous experience has taught them that a good board member comes to every meeting with two questions to ask of the paid staff person directing that agency. The first is "What are your goals for this agency?" After a discussion, frequently a refinement, and sometimes a redefinition of those goals, a reasonable level of agreement is reached on those goals. Ideally this will produce a consensus of support from the board, or at least an overwhelming majority.

This model works best when the board members and staff share many of the same values, when the board focuses on probable outcomes, not on means-to-an-end issues, when the agenda separates the trivial from the important, when the necessary information is available to all board members in advance of the meeting, when the board is more concerned with fulfilling the religious needs of people than with pleasing the staff, and when the board members understand and accept the fact that "the buck stops here," not at a congregational meeting or with the staff.

At this point the board members raise the second question, "What can we do to help turn those goals into reality?"

A translation of that definition of the role of the governing board in your church might cause the board members to raise these two questions: "Pastor, what do you believe the Lord is calling this congregation to be and to be doing in the days and months ahead?" (Note: This is not the same as asking, "Pastor, what do you want from us?") This might be followed by a period of serious reflection on the pastor's response in the context of the New Testament's statement about the nature and purpose of the worshiping community.

After the board has come to a common understanding on that first question, they can raise the second: "What can we do to turn that vision into reality?"

The pastor who is comfortable with this concept of the role of the governing board may respond to that first question with a carefully thought out statement on the vision or the challenge the pastor believes God has laid before this congregation. That could be followed by the question, "Now would you tell us how this compares with what you believe the Lord is calling us to be and do?" (Note: That is not the same as asking, "What do you want?")

After that discussion has come to an end and the board has asked that second question, the pastor should be prepared to describe what will be needed to turn that vision into reality. This could be followed by the question, "What is the best way to mobilize the necessary resources, or do you see a better way to do that?"

In this model the primary responsibility of the board is not to do all the work, but rather to make sure the work is done in a manner consistent with the self-identified role of this congregation and with the values, goals, priorities, and policies that have been adopted by that board. This model also requires the board to be able to trust both staff and committees.

This style of board meeting will be easier to carry out and will be more productive if the board includes fewer than a dozen members. The Bible tells us that when the size of the group reaches twelve, there is a good chance one will betray you and one will deny he or she ever knew you.

This alternative works best when the leaders, both volunteer and paid, share the following six assumptions. First, the primary responsibility of the board is not to control or supervise or oversee the work of the senior minister and the staff, but rather to cooperate with and support the staff and committees in designing and implementing ministry. Second, a substantial amount of authority is granted to committees and staff to initiate and implement. Third, the board is not expected to review and approve every detail, but rather to approve the general direction this congregation is headed, to define the parameters or boundaries of what is acceptable, and to identify and uphold fundamental organizational values. Any proposal that is compatible with the direction, parameters, and these organizational values usually receives routine approval. Fourth, the board can be trusted to act as representatives of the total membership. Therefore, it is neither necessary nor appropriate to refer specific proposals to a congregational vote. The congregation's primary responsibility is to elect representatives it can trust. In other words, and this is a crucial point, this alternative affirms a system of representative church government. Fifth, many of the matters that go before the congregation at a congregational meeting in smaller churches are resolved by the board in this system. Sixth, the focus of the annual congregational meeting in this system is not on "business" or on legislating, but rather on inspiration, proclamation of the gospel, celebration, reporting, enthusiastic singing, intercessory prayer, lifting up the vision of what the Lord is calling this congregation to be tomorrow, affirmation, visual communication, instrumental music, laughter, recognition of volunteers and of long-tenured members, and a fast pace.

Do not expect the annual meeting to be a legislative session that will make difficult decisions on controversial or divisive questions. Those issues should be studied and resolved within the committee system and the governing board. If the constitution requires it, a carefully prepared and fully documented recommendation may have to come before the congregational meeting for approval, but all the homework should have been completed earlier. If you are in doubt about the probable response by the annual meeting to a particular recommendation or proposal, it probably needs more work in committee or more time for people to reflect on it.

The annual meeting can be an effective place for sharing information, for adopting recommendations that have been properly processed by committees, for electing a slate of nominees for office, for celebrating victories, and for the affirmation of individuals and groups, but only in small churches is it an appropriate place to resolve complex or divisive issues.

A fifth alternative often is chosen by default when one or more of these conditions prevail: (1) a strong initiating senior pastor is replaced by a new minister who refuses to lead and who insists, "It doesn't matter what I want, I don't have any more wisdom than you, and I believe in a lay-run church"; (2) the congregation outgrows, in size and complexity, the system of governance and the leadership ability of the staff; (3) tradition and a desire to perpetuate the status quo have turned what once was a numerically growing church into a parish that is growing older and smaller; (4) the values, preferences, and religious needs of the members have changed, but the program continues on the assumption that next year will be 1952; (5) a deep and divisive quarrel between two influential staff members either immobilizes or polarizes the staff and the governing board; (6) a moral scandal erupts that involves a widely beloved staff member, and several leaders move to the sidelines until that is resolved; (7) the highly influential senior minister unofficially informs people, "In a few years I'll be leaving, but I'm not prepared to announce the date at this time," and thus becomes a lame duck; or (8) a deep rift finds the senior minister and the majority of the volunteer leaders on one side and a small but extremely articulate group of volunteer leaders plus a widely respected staff member on the other side.

The result often is institutional drift. Regardless of the system of governance, decisions are not implemented and goals that are mutually incompatible are proposed but not adopted because the decision-making system has been immobilized. A small but steady stream of ministry-oriented members quietly leave. Their departure might not be noticed, and thus their absence is rarely mentioned in official circles, but they are not replaced. That circle of volunteers becomes smaller and smaller, and individuals are asked to carry three or four major responsibilities. Frequently, the real issue, which is that this has become a passive, goalless, and drifting parish, is not discussed.[8] Instead, the discussions focus on the financial squeeze or the loss of a valued staff member or the shortage of volunteers or the decreasing number of new faces.

A sixth alternative is to make all staff members accountable to the senior minister and/or executive pastor and/or program director rather than to committees; hold the senior minister, executive pastor, and program director accountable to a governing board of ten or fewer members; charge the program committees with the oversight and continuity of program under the general oversight of the program director; and depend on ad hoc committees for change, innovation, discontinuity, new ministries, and one-time events.

A seventh alternative is consistent with the concept of individual entrepreneurial program members, described in chapter 4. This works well with a large governing board of twenty-five to sixty members; a senior minister with a far above average level of personal, professional, spiritual, and emotional security; an executive minister who also is an initiating leader; an exceptionally ambitious program director who is a skilled empire builder; and a crew of enthusiastic, gifted, creative, venturesome, trustworthy, productive, energetic, and happy program staff members.

Who runs that church?

The most frequently articulated answers one hears when visiting it are (1) the Holy Spirit, (2) no one, and (3) the cabinet, composed of the senior minister, the executive pastor, the program director, and the five- to seven-member executive committee of that large governing board.

The other common response is ''Who cares? The important issue is not control but doing ministry in harmony with God's will.''

CHAPTER SIX

Continuity and Succession

*"An institution is the lengthened
shadow of one man."*
—RALPH WALDO EMERSON

T he vast majority of small Protestant congregations in the United States and Canada are glued together by at least a half dozen of these twelve organizing principles: (1) faith in God as Creator and Jesus Christ as Savior; (2) denominational identity and polity; (3) kinship and friendship ties; (4) national, lingual, racial, or ethnic heritage; (5) real estate; (6) a distinctive place at one end or the other of the theological spectrum; (7) the shared experiences and memories of longtime members; (8) the Sunday school; (9) caring for one another; (10) a set of symbols and rituals that give meaning to life; (11) a twenty-year or longer pastorate; and/or (12) social class.

When two or three of those central organizing principles cease to be attractive to new generations of people and/or to newcomers to that community, these small congregations usually experience a decline in numbers.

Ten of the most common organizing principles that have helped to glue together the Sunday morning congregation include (1) excellent music, (2) inspiring preaching and memorable sermons, (3) a strong Sunday school, (4) denominational loyalties, (5) a high priority for missions, (6) effective pastoral care of the members, (7) sometimes a role as the most prestigious congregation in that community, (8) a long-tenured pastor who also is a widely known community leader, (9) a distinctive social class identity, and (10) that set of symbols and rituals that give meaning to life.

Few churches display all of these characteristics, but many of the great

Sunday morning congregations could claim seven or eight of them. In a few, their role was reinforced by a clearly defined claim to a virtual monopoly on one spot on the theological spectrum, often at the liberal end.

The generations to whom those organizing principles had the greatest appeal began to die off in substantial numbers during the 1960s and 1970s. Only a relatively small number of replacements could be found from among the younger generations. Gradually these Sunday morning congregations found themselves growing older and smaller. Sometimes the departure of that magnetic personality who had served for a decade or two or three as the senior minister appeared to hasten the pace of numerical decline. This pattern can be seen repeatedly in the "great" Protestant churches of New York City, Cleveland, Atlanta, St. Petersburg, Detroit, Buffalo, Chicago, Denver, Toronto, Los Angeles, and dozens of other cities.

The rapid numerical decline of so many of these large and famous congregations reminded observers of Emerson's observation that an institution is the lengthened shadow of one person. This has led a new generation of observers to predict that the megachurches of today will quickly fade away when that influential founding pastor departs.

While it is still too early to offer an ironclad and universal guarantee about the future, the early evidence suggests this analogy overlooks some of the differences between the big Sunday morning congregations of the 1950s and 1960s and the large seven-day-a-week churches of today.

Where Is the Continuity?

Perhaps the most significant difference is the matter of institutional continuity. The institutional continuity of the Sunday morning church of 1955 or 1965 often resided in the senior minister. When that individual departed, much of the institutional momentum and continuity also departed. The resulting vacuum often was followed by a disruptive decline in numbers. This helps to explain that remarkable decrease in the number of large United Methodist and Presbyterian congregations in Ohio, Wisconsin, Illinois, Iowa, California, Indiana, and other states between 1960 and 1985.

The departure of the senior pastor from that large Sunday morning Lutheran parish often was far less disruptive. In many of these parishes, a much larger part of the institutional continuity was in the sacraments, the liturgy, the national heritage, the symbols and rituals, that Lutheran identity, the denominational tradition, the culture, and the customs.

In a similar manner, the departure of that great preacher from the large Southern Baptist congregation often was less disruptive than when a similar change of senior ministers occurred in the Methodist or Presbyterian church down the street. For many large Southern Baptist churches, much of that institutional momentum and continuity was in the Cooperative Program, missions, the Sunday school, the Women's Missionary Union, music, the deacons, the Church Training Union, Sunday evening worship, Wednesday night prayer meeting, the state convention, camps, Lottie Moon, Annie Armstrong, Baptist colleges, and the Bible. When the preacher left, the house did not come tumbling down. Most of the pillars remained standing.

This discussion introduces two overlapping issues that are central to any discussion of the nature and future of the seven-day-a-week church.

Sources of Continuity in Large-Program Churches

For many participants in the life, ministry, and outreach of the seven-day-a-week church, the sense of continuity is not in the person of the senior pastor. For many of the people, the continuity is in that mutual support group that meets every Thursday evening or in an adult Sunday school class or in volunteering to staff the hunger commission or in the Mothers' Club that meets every Tuesday morning or in the staff and program of the Early Childhood Development Center or in weekly visits with persons in jail or in that early Saturday morning prayer and Bible study group or in serving as a Sunday school teacher or in that volleyball league or in the Board of Deacons or in the women's organization or in that group of five wise volunteer leaders who meet with the senior minister every Friday to minister to one another or in the ministry of music or in that high priority given to missions or in volunteering to work with one high school youth group.

In other words, much of that institutional continuity lies in the program, not in the sermons or the preacher in these churches.

Frequently, a second big slice of that continuity and momentum is in the high level of competence, commitment, and sense of community within that paid program staff. This point was stressed by the senior minister of one seven-day-a-week church who observed, "The only people we hire for our program staff are candidates who are more competent than I am.'' The higher the quality and the longer the tenure of the paid program staff, the less disruptive will be the departure of the senior minister.

Another senior minister affirmed this by explaining, ''A year after I arrived, I insisted we create a new position on the staff. This is our minister of preaching who preaches nearly every Sunday evening and at the early service about forty-five Sundays a year and takes my place at the second and third services whenever I'm out of town. I'm determined that this place is not going to fall apart when I leave.''

By contrast, in many Sunday morning churches it is assumed that most or all of the program staff should and will resign following the departure of the long-tenured senior minister. In more than a few churches, the call extended to the associate minister includes a provision that the call will automatically be terminated on the departure of that senior minister.

A more common approach for enhancing the institutional continuity within the paid program staff is by the nature of the assignments. Instead of building a dozen little isolated fiefdoms, one practice is to broaden staff responsibilities. One staff person, and this includes both lay and ordained program staff, is assigned to serve as both the ''pastor'' and the staff contact person with every class, group, choir, organization, board, committee, and circle. Thus the minister of music could serve as ''Our Pastor'' with one adult Sunday school class, one circle in the women's organization, one evening Bible study group, the chancel choir, the prison ministry, one volleyball team, and the volunteer staff in the nursery at the first Sunday morning service. This does not require attending every meeting of that group, but gives each ''mini-congregation'' its own representation at staff meetings and also broadens the base of continuity.

A third component of that redundant system for expanding the continuity beyond the senior minister often is in the volunteer leadership. Historically the most common examples of this have been in the volunteer superintendent of the Sunday school, the Elder Board, the trustees, the deacons, the officers of the women's organization, the treasurer, the volunteer youth counselors, and teachers in the church school.

A fourth source of continuity may be in the denominational identity. The people are glued into that parish in part by a loyalty to that congregation and also by an allegiance to that denomination and for what it stands. This is a stronger glue among people born before 1930 than it is with those born after 1945. In several religious traditions the continuity that was perpetuated by denominational loyalties was partially eroded by the denominational mergers of the 1955–90 era.

For many, but not all, large, full-service congregations, a big slice of the continuity is a product of the fact that this is a high-commitment church. High expectations are projected to those who ask to become members. In these high-commitment churches, the average attendance at Sunday morning worship usually is equivalent to 80 to 300 percent of the reported membership. When that high level of commitment is directed largely toward (1) Jesus Christ, (2) the ministry and outreach of that parish, and (3) a clearly stated belief system rather than to the senior minister, it is relatively easy for that pastor to be replaced by a successor. The two big exceptions, of course, are when (1) the expression of those three points of commitment really is in that senior minister and they have not been fully absorbed into the fabric of that parish, or (2) the successor undermines, neglects, or disowns one or more of those three points of commitment.

In other words, if the essence of that congregation is eroded when the senior minister is replaced, it is only reasonable to expect a large exodus.

A sixth source of continuity in the large full-service church often is in the high quality of the total ministry. The arrival of a new senior pastor does bring a new personality and a fresh approach to ministry. That may undercut the allegiance of those who identified with the predecessor rather than with the ministry of that parish. They may feel neglected and tempted to leave. Where can they go? Every church they visit during that period of temptation offers a lower quality ministry. This is obvious in the preaching, in the music, in the vitality of the worship experience, in the teaching ministry, in the announcements, in the weekday program, and in the group life. So they return "home."

This raises a widely ignored facet about the migration of church members. When interviewed, those churchgoers who switch from one congregation to another without that shift being motivated by a change in the place of residence almost always identify one or more benefits resulting from that change. The majority point to a more meaningful worship experience. A smaller group migrated in search of a more extensive program. The third group are grateful for the higher quality of the total program in their new church home. This helps to explain why most move from a numerically shrinking parish to a numerically growing church. What attracts them also attracts other church shoppers.

This point also explains why one of the top priorities of the most effective newly arrived pastors is not "calling on every member to discover how they see this church" or "maintaining everything just as I found it" or "not rocking the boat for at least a year." The top priority for these new arrivals is "How can I improve the quality of the ministry here?"

This discussion of quality as a source of continuity also helps to explain one of the big differences between those who leave and those who stay following the arrival of a new pastor. Those who stay usually place a high value on (1) the importance of friendship and kinship ties; (2) institutional loyalties; (3) participation in a group, class, committee, choir, task force, or circle; (4) geographical convenience; (5) denominational allegiance; and (6) the relationship with a program staff member (choir director, associate minister, youth counselor, etc.). Those who depart for another church usually place a high value on (1) the quality of worship in general and preaching in particular, (2) the need "to be fed spiritually," (3) missions and community outreach, (4) the teaching ministry, (5) the friendliness toward newcomers, and (6) the younger age of the members in the congregation that is their new church home.

The seventh point of continuity, which often eases succession, may be the most subtle, and it overlaps the factor of quality. This is the combination of goals and pace. Churches that display a clear goal orientation, as contrasted with drifting in a goalless manner, tend to be especially attractive to adult males. Likewise, those parishes with a comparatively fast pace of congregational life also tend to be more attractive than those that are drifting at a slow pace.

More important from the perspective of succession, however, is that the goal-driven and fast-paced congregation makes it relatively easy for a new senior minister to come on board without disrupting the sense of movement, continuity, and progress. When those goals were initiated by a partnership of program staff and volunteers and that parish is well along in the process of implementing them, that process provides useful continuity. By contrast, when the goals were initiated and solely owned by the recently departed senior pastor, that departure inevitably will create disruption and discontinuity.

Since most large full-service program churches are by definition goal-driven and must operate at a relatively fast pace, that eases the succession process.

The obvious exception, of course, is when the newly arrived senior minister displays little or no sympathy for those goals and insists on slowing the pace in order to set a new direction and formulate new goals consistent with that new direction. The source of that disaster is in the ministerial placement system, not in the large church.

The Power of the Congregational Culture

Another way of looking at this issue of continuity and succession is summarized in the concept of congregational culture. Every congregation that has been in existence for a decade or longer has developed a distinctive culture. This reflects a combination of tradition, the belief system, priorities, personalities, values, goals, widely shared experiences, denominational identity, size, language or nationality or racial or ethnic heritage, schedule, pace, polity, age of the members, level of commitment, theological stance, community image, social class, and similar factors.

The smoothest transitions in ministerial leadership occur when the new pastor is able to fit into that congregational culture easily, comfortably, and with few adjustments required of either congregation or new pastor. The smooth transition, however, is not always the best. A common example of a smooth transition may happen when the easy going, relaxed, fifty-seven-year-old minister who is looking forward eagerly to retirement comes to the aging, shrinking, and low-commitment church. As they grow older together, they can slow the pace, cut back on programming that no longer is needed, and enjoy the sunset.

A smooth transition may be what the members wanted, but that is not what that church needed!

When we move to the other end of the spectrum in the size of congregations, the question arises: What does the large full-service program church need when the time comes to look for a successor to the senior minister?

Two Directions

While this greatly oversimplifies a complex issue, two answers can be given to that question.

In most cases the *numerically growing* full-service church with a seven-day-a-week program probably should seek a smooth transition and look for a successor who will fit easily, comfortably, and quickly into that congregational culture.

In most cases the *numerically shrinking* full-service program church probably should seek a successor who is a creative, initiating leader who sees the need to improve the quality of the total ministry, who is a skilled agent of intentional change, who believes in seven-day-a-week programming, who displays a strong future orientation, and who knows how to build and sustain the coalitions and alliances essential for permanent changes.

The success of these transitions often evokes comments such as these: "I don't see why we have to change everything all at once." "Some of us are satisfied with how things are going. Why do we have to make so many changes?" "It used to be I knew nearly everyone who came to the eleven o'clock service; now with this new schedule I hardly know anyone." "Who forced Reverend Soandso to resign?"

Who Are the Best Successors?

This discussion of the sources of continuity, of the power of the congregational culture, and of the occasional need for a disruptive transition is offered as a context for looking at the choice of a successor.[1] What are the qualities we seek in a successor for our departing senior minister? One answer, of course, is excellent character, outstanding competence as a preacher, an attractive personality, ability to relate comfortably and effectively with a large program staff, slightly on the malnourished side, a deep solid Christian commitment, articulate, widely read, good health, and beautiful children.

Those are useful indicators if the process of selecting a successor is to resemble a beauty contest.

A better beginning point would be to look at the sources of continuity in the large full-service church. This could produce this long sentence: "We are seeking a new senior minister who understands the importance of seven-day-a-week programming, who places a premium on a highly competent staff, who appreciates the role of volunteers in the large church, who believes in the high commitment church that projects high expectations of everyone, including the senior minister, who will want to enhance the quality of our ministry and knows how to do it, who will be in complete agreement with the basic direction this congregation is going, who will understand our unique congregational culture and feel comfortable with it, and who will bring a strong goal orientation to ministry."

The best successor for the senior minister in the large program church will fit that description.

Where Will We Find That Person?

In their search for a successor to that recently departed great pulpiteer with the winsome personality, the Sunday morning churches of the 1950s usually turned to another, somewhat smaller Sunday morning church. They offered a promotion from this top minor league team to the major leagues. This offer usually included a more attractive compensation package, a larger staff, a better office, a reserved off-street parking space, four weeks of study leave in addition to vacation time every summer, and other fringe benefits.

The usual result followed one of two patterns. In the success stories, the new senior minister said, "I've never been the pastor of a church as large as this one before, but I'm determined to learn what I need to know. With God's help, we'll make this work."

In the second pattern the successor came in and observed, "I've never been the senior minister of a church as large as this one before, so I'll keep on doing what I was doing that caused me to be invited to come here." The usual result was that within five years (1) that successor had departed and/or (2) that congregation had shrunk substantially in size.

The moral of that story is reflected in the words of the traveling salespersons of 1900, "You've got to know the territory."

If the situation calls for a smooth transition, an affirmation of the current role and direction, and perpetuating the basic style of ministry, experience suggests that the best chances for a smooth transition in the very large program church will come from among these alternatives:

1. The ordained son of the long-tenured senior pastor, who has been on the staff as an associate minister for at least seven years, becomes the successor.
2. The ordained son-in-law of the long-tenured senior pastor, who has been the number-one associate minister to his father-in-law for several years, becomes the successor.

145

3. The long-tenured associate minister, who may have never served on the staff of any other church, becomes the successor.

This range of choices may surprise the reader as much as it surprised this writer when research revealed that pattern. Whenever research reveals a surprise, a useful response is to ask, "How come? Why?"

On reflection, the obvious explanation is that in each case the successor knew the territory. The successor had been thoroughly socialized into the culture of that large congregation and was fully supportive of the values, traditions, goals, priorities, and theological stance of that parish. Furthermore, the successor knew the key volunteer leaders and was trusted by those influential volunteer leaders—otherwise the invitation would not have been issued. It goes without saying, of course, that the successor has to be a competent preacher.

The next pair of success stories in the smooth transitions are more predictable.

4. The gifted young minister, who has been serving as the associate pastor of a larger full-service congregation with an even more extensive weekday program, becomes the new senior minister.
5. The senior minister of another large full-service program church is invited to become the successor.

If the situation calls for considerable change, rather than reinforcing continuity, the success stories often fit one of these five patterns.

1. The senior minister of a numerically growing larger program church is persuaded to accept the challenge.
2. A pastor who left the position of senior minister of a large full-service church to serve in the denominational bureaucracy for several years is persuaded to accept the challenge.
3. The senior minister of a large full-service church in a different religious tradition comes as the successor.
4. The senior minister of a newer, smaller, but rapidly growing church is selected to become the successor.
5. The gifted and relatively young associate minister of a larger full-service church from a different religious tradition becomes the successor.

All ten of these alternatives contrast sharply with the conventional wisdom that insists that the road to becoming the senior minister of a large program church in urban America that is reaching and serving large numbers of people born after 1955 should begin by spending one or two pastorates in small rural congregations serving people born before 1940.

All ten of these alternatives reflect the importance of "knowing the territory," of being comfortable with the distinctive culture of the large program church, and of being comfortable serving in a large and complex parish setting.

CHAPTER SEVEN

Clouds and Questions

D uring the Great Depression of the 1930s Americans were extremely cost conscious, and retail trade became highly competitive. Grocers found that one means of cutting costs was to abandon the old practice of a clerk's bringing each item to the counter while the customer waited. Grocery stores were redesigned to encourage the customer to pick up the groceries in a basket and carry them to the cash register. This reduction in the size of the payroll enabled the grocer to cut prices. By 1940, a year before Pearl Harbor, 10 percent of all groceries were sold in these self-service supermarkets. That proportion tripled to 30 percent by 1950 and doubled to 60 percent during the next five years. By 1960 supermarkets accounted for 70 percent of all grocery store sales. By 1980 supermarkets represented only 11 percent of all grocery stores but sold 70 percent of the groceries. If one counts customers or volume of business, supermarkets dominate the retailing of groceries. If one counts stores, the small convenience stores with extended hours are twice as numerous as supermarkets. Even more numerous, however, are the small neighborhood grocery stores, often operated by one family, that serve a limited number of customers.

A similar pattern can be seen in American Protestantism with the emergence of what some call the "superchurches" and what are identified in this book as the large full-service churches with a seven-day-a-week program. Approximately one-fifth of all churches account for one-half of all people worshiping with a Protestant congregation on the typical Sabbath.

The number of small "Mom and Pop" or family-run neighborhood grocery stores dropped by approximately 20 percent during the 1980s. In a similar manner literally thousands of small neighborhood-oriented Protestant churches also closed during the 1980s.

In both cases this was due in part to the pressures of competition and the disappearance of older generations of customers and members born during the first third of the twentieth century. Many from those older generations were willing to accept a more limited range of choices in favor of the personal service, the intimacy, the familiarity, and the friendliness of that smaller institution. Some of these favorite customers and members have moved away. Many have died, and a few have switched to a larger institution.

The first parallel for the Protestant church scene is in that sales figure. Despite the increasing attractiveness of supermarkets of all types, they still have not been able to go beyond approximately 70 percent of the market. Nearly 30 percent of grocery store sales still are being made by the convenience stores, the small cooperative stores, the family-owned and operated neighborhood groceries, the small bakeries, the specialty stores, and the superettes. A reasonable guess is that perhaps one-eighth of all Protestant churchgoers in the United States in the year 2012 will choose a congregation that averages fewer than 100 at worship, and another one-fourth will pick a church that averages between 100 and 200 at worship. (In 1990 approximately 42 percent of all the people worshiping with an Evangelical Free congregation were attending a church that averaged less than 200 at worship. By contrast two-thirds of those worshiping with a Church of the Nazarene congregation were in a church that averaged fewer than 200 at worship as were 62 percent of those worshiping with a United Methodist congregation, 64 percent of those attending a United Church of Christ worship service, and 41 percent of those worshiping with a Lutheran Church-Missouri Synod parish.)

A second parallel also can be found in the recent history of supermarkets. During the 1980s, the number of supermarkets in the United States held steady at slightly over 26,000. The number of "conventional" supermarkets, however, decreased by nearly one-third, while the number of "superstores" doubled, the number of huge "warehouse" stores also doubled, and the number of "superware-house" and "hypermarket" outlets increased fortyfold. These changes have been fed by the increase in the number of shoppers who are willing to travel longer distances, endure greater traffic congestion, and invest more time in order to benefit from a broader range of choices, lower prices, and the convenience of one-stop shopping. The market share of the conventional supermarkets dropped from 56 percent of all grocery sales in 1980 to 30 percent in 1988. The market share of the various kinds of huge supermarkets nearly tripled from 14 percent in 1980 to 39 percent in 1988. The giant superstores have been taking market share from the conventional supermarket.[1]

How do these trends speak to the large full-service church with a seven-day-a-week program? The parallels are provocative.

While the full-service churches began to appear about a generation later than the self-service supermarkets, both have appealed largely to the same market—the generations born after 1930, and especially the generations born after 1940. Both have had limited success in reaching those younger adults who seek a store or church that specializes in a high-quality, but narrowly defined, niche.

Both recognize and affirm the need to draw people from a ten- to thirty-mile radius. Neither can survive with a walk-in neighborhood constituency. Both understand the need for a large parcel of land at a highly visible and convenient location with an abundance of off-street parking. Both accept the need to take advantage of contemporary marketing principles. Both recognize that their future lies in being responsive to the needs of their clientele. Both appeal to the two-car, two-income family as well as to adults without regard to marital status. Both are consistent with the strong "consumerism" of contemporary American society. Both operate on the assumption that the quality of their current performance, rather than inherited loyalties or brand-name allegiance or geographical proximity is what will cause this week's first-time visitors to return next week. Both evoke the same reaction in many of the first-time visitors born before 1920—the size, scale, array of choices, pace, and extravagance are perceived as overwhelming. Both can be found in largely black sections of the inner city as well as in suburbia, although the company name on the building may not be the same in both places.

Both understand who is their real competition. Their real competition is not the small institution organized by a couple of immigrants to serve an immigrant population from the Pacific Rim. Their real competition is not the small, intimate, friendly institution that has a special appeal to many of those born before 1935. Their serious competition is not the speciality operation a mile away that has carved out a distinctive niche to serve a narrow and precisely defined slice of the population. The real competition comes from (1) the new big institution that is seeking to reach the shoppers who have yet to settle into the habit of going to the same place week after week and (2) the even bigger institution that can offer an even broader range of high quality choices.[2]

To be more precise, the competition for tomorrow's new members for the large program church is not the small neighborhood churches (except in reaching the generations born before World War II); it is other large, attractive, full-service churches with a seven-day-a-week program. This introduces the first of several clouds on the horizon.

Eleven Clouds

The first is symbolized by the building that once housed a supermarket but is now occupied by a videotape rental store or some other use. That supermarket either closed or relocated because it could not keep up with the competition from that building at that location.

Likewise scores of today's program churches will either close or relocate. In some cases the building is too small. For others the off-street parking is inadequate. (In the Sunday morning church the leaders evaluated the adequacy of off-street parking in terms of Sunday morning needs. In the seven-day-a-week church the critical question is whether the available parking for weekday and evening programing is adequate, convenient, safe, and easy to use.) For many, the combination of an obsolete building on an inadequate site at an inconvenient location motivated the decision to relocate. In other words, the limitations of the present physical facilities mean some of today's large program churches will not be competitive tomorrow as new, larger, and more attractive full-service congregations come on the scene. A small number of program churches have responded to the issue of "relocate or remain" by answering, "Both." They have chosen to become multi-site churches with two or three or four sites under one administrative umbrella with one staff.

The second cloud may never produce rain, but it is too early to tell. Will the generations born after 1968 be as comfortable in large, complex, and impersonal institutions as their parents are today? Perhaps as many as one-third of the 1968–81 generation resemble their grandparents more than their parents. Will this slice of the younger generation, like many of those born before 1935, prefer smaller churches?

A third cloud parallels the current boom in the number of warehouse, superwarehouse, and hypermarket grocery stores. Will that trend be matched by an equivalent increase in the number of Protestant congregations averaging over 2,000 at worship? Contemporary evidence confirms that trend. If it continues, the competition will be more severe for the full-service churches now averaging 500 to 1,200 at worship.

More significant, perhaps, is the role of the senior minister in the very large church. History supports the generalization that the larger the size of the congregation, the more disruptive is the premature departure of the pastor. As was pointed out in the previous chapter, this generalization does not always apply in the very, very large program churches. The question remains, however, whether many of today's full-service congregations averaging 500 to 1,200 at worship will be able to survive both increased competition and the departure of that senior pastor who transformed this from a Sunday morning church into a seven-day-a-week church.

Overlapping these questions is a fourth cloud. Will the supply of senior ministers who are both superb preachers and effective initiating leaders be adequate to meet that growing demand? One of the most effective means of sharply reducing worship attendance in the large church is for the new senior minister to be a weak, dull, boring, and uninspiring preacher and/or to be an inept leader. Will the next generation of highly qualified pastors be sufficiently numerous to meet that demand? Will they come largely from the long-established theological seminaries or from new sources?

Equally important, will today's large full-service churches be able to produce the necessary number of competent and committed program specialists needed to meet the rapidly increasing demand?

A fifth cloud reflects one of the great differences between superchurches and supermarkets. Supermarkets attract customers in part because they benefit from an economy of scale. The larger the volume, the lower the unit costs. By contrast, large American Protestant churches are high unit cost operations. In 1991 the typical Protestant church averaging 150 at worship could pay all of its bills if the offerings averaged $10 to $20 per worshiper per Sunday. In the typical full-service congregations, expenditures often average out to $25 to $50 per Sunday per worshiper. (An increasing proportion of those expenditures now come from user fees rather than the offering plate.) Will that demand for both choices and quality price some of today's large program churches out of the market?

At least a few readers will insist that the most ominous cloud on the horizon reflects a common tendency among all long-established Protestant churches. This is to dilute the emphasis on being responsive to the religious and personal needs of new generations or potential future members by giving a higher priority to (a) the desires of the long-tenured members, (b) institutional survival, (c) denominational priorities, and/or (d) the desire to do yesterday over again. "What brought you here may not keep you here" applies to large churches as well as to other clientele-oriented enterprises. Too often the biggest enemy turns out to be "our last great new program." Our most attractive maps entice us to go into the territory that was fully explored yesterday. No one can supply an equally detailed and attractive map to guide the journey into the future. Repeating yesterday always looks safer than creating a new tomorrow.

The seventh cloud hangs only over those congregations with strong denominational ties. This is the threat of a denominational split or polarization, which can encourage a destructive diversion of resources that will undermine ministry and outreach.

An eighth cloud appears only occasionally, but when it rains, it pours discouragement, disruption, disillusionment, and division and is almost always a diversion from ministry and outreach. These depressing consequences often come out of the moral failure of the senior minister or a widely beloved and highly effective program staff member. Once again the larger the size of the congregation, the more disruptive are these unfortunate episodes.

The ninth cloud is the product of an excessively ambitious building committee that sacrifices program space needs and/or off-street parking in order to construct a magnificent sanctuary "large enough that we can return to only one worship service on Sunday morning." When implemented, this goal often creates a set of new and difficult problems. The most highly visible may be a huge mortgage that subverts the purpose of that congregation into raising money to meet the payments.[3] The second is that the more diverse the membership, the more difficult it is to design one worship experience that will meet everyone's religious needs. The third, and the most subtle, is scale. Thus this congregation may have a sanctuary that can seat 1,600 at one service, but accommodate only 500 in Sunday school with off-street parking for 200 cars and office space for three full-time program staff members. A design of those proportions may have been appropriate for the Sunday morning church of 1954, but not for the full-service parish of 1994!

When the tenth cloud moves onto the horizon, it usually is a product of (a) the confidence and authority vested in the senior minister and staff described in chapter 4 and (b) the doctrine of original sin. The operational term for this cloud is "an absence of adequate accountability." Who will hold the senior minister and the staff accountable?

It used to be assumed that a congregational board of elders or deacons or a denominational committee or officials would hold pastors accountable for their actions and teachings. Those systems are being eroded and are less and less effective. As deeply held convictions have been replaced by the belief that one person's opinion should carry as much weight as anyone else's opinion, pastors have become more reluctant to hold one another accountable.

Increasingly, the real system of accountability is the marketplace. The erosion of institutional loyalties, especially among those born after World War II, has made it easy for unhappy churchgoers to seek another church home. Today's system of accountability is being administered through the feet and pocketbook. The boring sermon, the uninspired worship service, the absence of initiating leadership by the pastor, the questionable moral behavior of a paid staff member, or the earned distrust of the administration of the finances motivates many people to disappear silently. This is not a new concept in our society. What is new is that the marketplace is now the most widely used system of evaluation by younger churchgoers. Accountability for the megachurch is determined by whether or not the people keep coming and giving. The absence of a reliable system of accountability that can intervene before a problem grows into a crisis can undermine any congregation, but the very large program churches are especially vulnerable.

The downside of this, of course, is the tendency to depend more on the market than on the mission. Should a church formulate its priorities and design its ministries in response to the expressed needs of people? Or should the driving force be the Bible, the creeds, traditions, and priorities of the pastors? To some, the popularity and success of today's very large congregations represent a dangerous concession to the rampant consumerism characteristic of contemporary American society.

Finally, the most threatening, but inadequately discussed, cloud may turn out to be the proliferation of restrictions by municipal authorities on the use of land for religious purposes.[4] Among the most common criticisms of today's very large program churches is that they own too much land that should be on the tax roll and they generate too much traffic.

How much land should any one congregation be allowed to own? Experience suggests a minimum of one acre for every one hundred people at worship (combined attendance for all services) on Sunday morning. That means the congregation averaging 1,500 at the early service and 2,500 at the second service needs forty acres of land. That is a *minimum!* In a growing number of municipalities, however, the requirements for off-street parking, setbacks, landscaping, traffic circulation, storm water control, and floor-to-ground-area ratios may require fifty to sixty acres. An increasing number of local governments, moreover, are adopting legislation that limits the amount of land any one congregation can own to twenty or thirty or forty acres. The constitutionality of these ordinances has yet to be tested in the United States Supreme Court, but their adoption clearly reflects an anti-mega-church value system of the local authorities.

Sometime during the 1990s, the United States Supreme Court will be asked to rule on the constitutionality of these restrictions. That decision, rather than the marketplace, may decide the future of the very large seven-day-a-week program churches.

Unanswered Questions

In addition to these clouds, several other questions float to the surface when the discussion turns to the future of the full-service church. The first of these, and by far the most complex, reflects the ambiguity in and absence of clarity in that term *full service*. What does *full service* mean? Obviously this term embraces corporate worship, intercessory prayer, Bible study, community ministries, affirmation and celebration, Christian education, nurture, fellowship, administration of the sacraments and other rituals, social action, mutual support groups, missions, challenging people to express their faith in and through this worshiping community, evangelism, eating together, pastoral care, symbols, music, caring for one another, a concern for peace and social justice, transmitting the faith from one generation to the next, choices, and teaching a full expression of stewardship.

What else belongs in that definition? This question can be illustrated by six examples.

A Congregational Health-Care System?

The first full-service health clinic in an American public school was founded in Dallas, Texas, in 1970. During the next fourteen years the idea spread slowly across the nation and by 1984 the number had grown to 31. During the next six years that number grew fivefold to 162. Today it is no longer the controversial issue it was in 1980. The inability of millions of families to provide adequate health care for their children has motivated educators to meet a need once provided by families. The menace of drug abuse, the increased level of violence in society, and the problem of teenage pregnancies have won many converts to this cause.

A parallel movement to encourage churches to be concerned with the total health of the individual has been spearheaded by Dr. Granger Westberg. This remarkable crusade has motivated hundreds of congregations to accept that challenge. One result is a growing acceptance of the concept that the health of the people should be a central concern of every parish.

One operational expression of this commitment is the parish nurse.[5] Today the staffs of more than four hundred congregations include a parish nurse or a minister of health. A second operational expression of this commitment is the Health Cabinet or committee, which is charged with promoting the healing ministry of that congregation.[6] A third is the sharp increase in the number of congregations that schedule a healing service every week. A fourth, and by far the most sophisticated, is the Congregational Health Partnership, involving the parish as an organization, the members, and various health-care providers.

Will the definition of a full-service church in 1999 include a parish nurse on the program staff, a wellness committee, and a partnership with other health care providers?

Where Will Our Children Go to School?

The second example raises one of the most divisive issues in Western history. What values and traditions should elementary schools seek to reinforce and perpetuate? In several nations in Europe the clear answer was social class differences. Upper-class children were educated in one system, while a different system was provided for working-class children. This concept was largely, but not completely, rejected in America.

Instead of designing an educational system on the basis of social class, three other conceptual frameworks have been followed in the United States.[7] The easiest to describe is the school system designed to teach, reinforce, and perpetuate the values and traditions of a particular religious faith. This category is illustrated by the thousands of Lutheran, Roman Catholic, Seventh Day Adventist, Presbyterian, Episcopal, Christian Reformed, Congregational, Methodist, and Baptist schools that have operated in the United States.[8]

One example of that approach to educating children was represented by the Reverend George Atkinson, a Congregational minister. He was sent to the Oregon territory by the American Home Missionary Society in the middle of the nineteenth century to create "churches, schools, whatever would benefit humanity—temperance, virtue, the industrial, mental, moral, and religious training of the young, and the establishment of society upon sound principles by means of institutions of religion and learning." In 1849 Atkinson persuaded the governor and the legislature to create a system of public schools. Subsequently Atkinson became the first school commissioner for Clackamas and Multnomah Counties. He continued, however, to establish new private Christian academies. Atkinson and scores of other Protestant ministers strongly advocated that public schools be pan-Protestant institutions. For them, the critical distinction was between Roman Catholic and Protestant schools, both private and public, not between public and private institutions. While speaking to the National Education Association's convention in 1888, Atkinson urged teachers to use the Bible as a textbook in public schools.[9] That admonition was not seen as inappropriate, since nineteen years earlier the National Teachers Association, the forerunner of the NEA, had adopted a resolution declaring, "The Bible should not only be studied, venerated and honored as a classic for all ages, peoples, and languages . . . but devotionally read, and its precepts inculcated in all the common schools of the land.''[10]

While both the pietistic Protestants and the Roman Catholics agreed that Christianity should be taught in the schools, they could not agree on the content and form. Since Protestants controlled the public schools in nearly all counties, that meant the Catholics had to build their own alternative system. They did. And they did it quickly and at great sacrifice. By 1890 their parochial schools reported a combined enrollment of 626,496, compared to 12.5 million in public elementary schools and 1.3 million in non-Catholic private schools. (For comparison purposes, in 1988 the enrollment in Catholic elementary schools was 1.9 million—down from 4.5 million in 1965—compared to 2.2 million in non-Catholic private elementary schools.)

A second conceptual framework for designing an educational system is to see it as an extension of the family. The Latin phrase *in loco parentis* expressed this. The school is expected to carry out the will of the parents and to teach, reinforce, inculcate, transmit, and perpetuate the values of the family.[11] For millions of children, the American public elementary schools of the nineteenth and early twentieth centuries followed this orientation.

In many rural communities in the late nineteenth century, the tax-supported public schools combined these first two designs into one. In three counties in Wisconsin, for example, Belgian immigrants controlled the public schools, and French was the language for both teachers and students.[12] In many more communities German immigrants controlled the local public school district. German was the language used in the classroom, and Lutheranism was the religion that was taught.

More common, however, was the Catholic or Lutheran parochial school that sought to transmit a compatible and mutually reinforcing combination of culture, moral values, ethical behavior, and religious beliefs.

Many of today's nonsectarian private schools were created to transmit the culture and values of one generation to the next.

A third orientation calls for the public schools to reflect and implement the values and goals of a democratic society. The schools are expected to be an equalizing or compensatory force that will be of particular benefit to children who come from a disadvantaged background. The public school in the United States, according to this perspective, should be a vehicle for upward mobility for the poor, a transmitter of democratic values, and a means of socializing children into the mainstream of American society.

In the German immigrant community in rural Wisconsin in 1910, the family, the Lutheran parish, and the Lutheran parochial school were mutually reinforcing institutions in the transmission of a religious tradition, a Germanic culture, a Christian value system, and ethical behavior norms. The high degree of homogeneity in these three institutions minimized conflict.

Likewise in the one-room public school in Wisconsin in 1930, which often was taught by a teacher reared in that community and graduated from that school five or six years earlier, there was a high level of agreement on values, goals, culture, and methods. Typically that school was governed by three parents who had been elected to serve as the officers for that district. The values taught in the home and the church were reinforced in that school.

As recently as 1930, for example, the one-teacher school accounted for 149,282 of the 238,306 public elementary schools in the United States.

Thirty years later, the schools in the United States entered into a period of great turmoil and conflict that still continues. Which set of values should prevail? Those held by the parents? By the youth culture of the 1960s? By the state legislatures? By the state and federal courts? By the teachers? By the administrators? By liberal Protestant leaders? By evangelical Protestant leaders? By the university schools of education? By the officials in the state department of public instruction? By Roman Catholic leaders? By self-identified advocates for children and youth? By the local school board? Out of this conflict came several developments. One was the segregationist academies founded in the 1956–65 era. A second was the creation of countless "alternative" schools. A third was the organization in the 1960s and 1970s of hundreds of private Christian schools by theologically conservative churches. A fourth was the recognition in the 1980s that the large central city systems were offering little assistance to children from disadvantaged black families. A fifth was a drop, for the first time in American history, in the rate of graduation from high school. In 1940 the number of high school graduates was equal to 51 percent of the number of seventeen year olds. By 1960 that rate had climbed to 65 percent, and it peaked at 77 percent in 1970. By 1980 it was down to 71.4 percent.

Another result was a new wave of interest in private Christian day schools. This new wave was led, not by Catholics and Lutherans, but by churches that did not have a tradition of Christian elementary schools. Among the leaders in this new wave of Christian day schools are black congregations in the central city, urban congregations affiliated with the liberal Protestant denominations, scores of new and rapidly growing evangelical churches seeking to reach parents with upward mobility ambitions for their children, and a wide range of large seven-day-a-week program churches serving parents born after 1950. These parents are not seeking a segregationist academy. They want a school for their children that teaches the same moral and ethical values the parents are attempting to transmit in the home. They do not seek a "value-free" education for their children. They seek a school that affirms, reinforces, models, teaches, and transmits Christian values.[13] Will the congregations seeking to reach new generations of parents of young children have to amend their 1998 definition of a full-service church to include a Christian day school?

A Home for Home Schoolers?

A third, and overlapping, example is a product of the recent rapid increase in the number of parents who choose to educate their children at home. Much of that increase consists of well-educated, socially and politically liberal parents who display serious reservations about contemporary public education and who are concerned about the transmission of values.[14] A growing, but still modest, number of churches have created a partnership with these parents to provide structured socialization activities and events on four or five afternoons every week. Will the definition of a full-service church in 1997 include ministries with home schoolers?[15]

Who Cares for the Children?

Many observers have become convinced that contemporary American society provides a barren environment for the rearing of healthy, competent, and well-adjusted children.[16]

In early 1991, for example, the Committee for Economic Development issued a report, "The Unfinished Agenda—A New Vision for Child Development and Education." This was the third time in six years that this group of business leaders had called for increased help for children. The 1991 report declared: "We are jeopardizing America's survival as a free and prosperous society and condemning much of a new generation to lives of poverty and despair." Those are strong words.

The present situation is a product of dozens of factors, including the deterioration of the family, the excessive emphasis now being placed on individualism and individual self-fulfillment, the delegation of an unprecedented number of responsibilities for the rearing of children to the schools, the growth in the size and the centralization of authority in several public institutions, the impact of television and the media, and the bias in public policy toward the elderly (the past) rather than toward children (the future).

Literally thousands of churches have begun to attack this issue with a variety of programs. These include nursery schools, latch-key programs, parenting classes, family life centers, and a countless number of other efforts. Will the definition of a full-service church in 1996 include a full-scale seven-day-a-week ministry with children or with families that include young children?

Where Should We Eat?

A fifth example also reflects the changing societal scene. The causes include the longer life expectancy of mature adults, lowering the age of retirement from the labor force, the doubling in the number of one-person households from 11 million in 1970 to over 23 million in 1991, the increasing number of people who prefer an earlier hour for worship on Sunday morning, the postponement of first marriage, the sharp increase in the number of people who eat out, the drop in the rate of remarriage after divorce or widowhood, the increase in the proportion of people born after 1950 who will never marry, and the acceptance by many Protestants of Saturday evening worship as an alternative to Sunday morning.

One product of those and other changes is the rapid increase in the number of churches that begin the Sunday morning schedule with breakfast. A second is the Wednesday evening program built around the central focus of eating together. A third is the Sunday noon meal for first-time visitors, young adults, folks of all ages who live alone, and empty nest couples. A fourth is the luncheon two or three days a week for retirees. A fifth is the recognition that one way to increase attendance for any special event is to begin with a meal. A sixth is the increasing number of churches that combine a meal, corporate worship, adult learning opportunities, and fellowship in the Saturday evening schedule.

Will the definition of a full-service church in 1995 include the preparation and serving of meals on seven to fifteen occasions every week?

Can Fun Be Ministry?

The last example has the greatest visibility in the Southeast and West, but it is spreading quietly and remarkably rapidly. This is the inclusion of sports, athletics, and recreation as an integral component of that seven-day-a-week program for fifty-two weeks a year. The motivations range from offering more intergenerational events (the Saturday afternoon father-daughter roller skating party) to a recognition of the importance of exercise to overcoming anonymity to creating additional entry points for tomorrow's new members to strengthening family ties to assimilating new members to increasing adult male participation. This also is highly compatible with the first example of making the church a wellness center as well as with a greater emphasis on children's ministries.

Will the definition of a full-service church in 1994 include a large-scale athletic exercise and recreation program? Will the minister of recreation be listed along with the minister of health, the minister of music, the minister of missions and outreach, the minister of community ministries, the minister of education, the minister of children's programming (or director of ministries with families that include young children), the minister of pastoral care, and the minister of fellowship and food services as an essential program staff position in the full-service church?

Generalist or Specialist?

That last question raises the issue of resources, including money. How many congregations can afford that many specialized program staff members? It also raises another of these puzzling questions: Will the program churches of 1999 seek to offer a comprehensive range of ministries and activities? Or will they specialize? One alternative could be the church that offers the full range of traditional ministries and also specializes in a range of events, programs, and activities designed for families with young children. Another might specialize in developing a comprehensive health partnership. A third might concentrate on a seven-day-a-week recreation and sports ministry. A fourth might focus on serving home schoolers living within a twenty-five or thirty mile radius. A fifth might offer a Christian day school as one component of a much larger teaching ministry.

Specialization would be a means of solving the problem of competition for limited resources among a growing number of competing demands. Specialization also would be consistent with what is happening in dozens of other places in our society. Several of the oldest and largest insurance companies in the United States have abandoned their traditional full-service approach in favor of a narrower focus on a few specialties. Similar patterns can be seen in book publishing, in the practice of law and medicine, and in the manufacture of automobiles. Market segmentation also is a marketing rule with most home builders, restaurant owners, magazine publishers, and many community colleges. Instead of attempting to be all things to all people, the decision was made to specialize in one precisely defined niche. Will the full-service churches follow that path?

The big drawback is that people change. We already know that one way to create an articulate lobby for a Christian day school is to extend the nursery school through kindergarten. If it is a high-quality program, next year some parents will insist that the program be expanded to include first grade. The following year they will want it to include second grade.

Carving out a narrowly defined niche and specializing in that one area of ministry does not make everyone happy. "As long as we have a gym for the day school, why don't we call a minister of recreation to build that up?"

"I'm all in favor of the Early Childhood Development Center, and we really benefited from it. But our youngest child is now eleven, and I think we need to build up the youth program." "A logical expansion of our Christian day school would be to serve the home schoolers."

How does the self-identified full-service church say, "No, we don't do that," and still defend the image of being a full-service church?

How Big?

In 1950 informed observers would have laughed at anyone who predicted, "Within forty years we'll have dozens of Protestant churches that average over 3,000 at worship. We'll also see churches that have 60 to 150 acres of land. Some of those congregations will include a university, a retirement center, a nursing home, a twelve-grade school plus kindergarten, and a children's home."

No one anticipated that the 1990s would bring Protestant congregations that average 6,000 to 14,000 at worship every weekend. That would have been as credible as the prediction in 1940 that in three decades we would see state universities with 30,000 students on one campus.[17]

How large will the full-service Protestant churches be in the year 2030? The only reliable answer is "No one knows."

Three developments of the past half century suggest the ceiling has not been reached. The first trend can be seen in the increasing number of churches that include more than a thousand members. For example, in 1950 only 1,019 Southern Baptist congregations reported a thousand or more members. By 1972 that figure had more than doubled to nearly 2,200. In 1989 a total of 2,941 Southern Baptist congregations reported a thousand or more members. It also is worth noting that 10 percent of the 800 largest congregations in the Southern Baptist Convention in 1989 were organized in 1959 or later. The post-1960 era also brought the organization of thousands of other very large churches. Many of these do not carry a denominational identity, while others are affiliated with the Assemblies of God, the Evangelical Free Church, one of the several Presbyterian denominations, the Church of the Nazarene, The United Methodist Church, one of the Lutheran denominations, or some other denomination. (It should be noted that this rising tide did not lift all of the ships in the harbor evenly. In 1988 The United Methodist Church reported 1,315 congregations with a thousand or more members, down sharply from the combined total of 1,816 for the two predecessor denominations in 1965.)

The second trend can be seen at the other end of the size scale. Long-established smaller congregations averaging fewer than a hundred at worship are experiencing increasing difficulty in being able to attract, challenge, provide an adequate compensation package, and keep a competent full-time resident pastor who can help that congregation attract new generations of younger members. As a result the majority of long-established small Protestant congregations are growing older and smaller.

This parallels what has been happening in the retail sales of groceries, to return to the opening illustration of this chapter. The very big are growing at the expense of the big. The big full-service churches—and the huge grocery stores—are attracting a disproportionate share of the people born after 1945. The very largest grocery stores doubled their market share in the 1980–88 era. While the analogy has limitations, it does suggest that full-service churches averaging 1,200 or more at worship continue to attract those who twenty years earlier would have been completely satisfied with the scope of the program and the range of choices offered by the congregation that averaged 450 to 700 at worship.

SUPERMARKET SALES

Percent Distribution of Sales

	1980	1988
Conventional		
Supermarkets.	73%	43%
Superstores.......	18%	30%
Warehouses.....	4%	13%
Others*...........	5%	14%

*Combination food and drug, superware-houses and hypermarkets. Source: *Statistical Abstract of the United States 1990*, p. 774.

The third trend is that the journey to work is lengthening. The suburbanization of the American population during the 1950s and 1960s lengthened the distance from place of residence to the place of work. The desire of many to "live in the country" and still have a city paycheck accelerated this trend during the 1970s and 1980s. For many adults the yardstick for measuring how far is an acceptable distance to church is not minutes or miles. It is the journey to work. As the journey to work gets longer, it is more acceptable to drive ten or twenty or thirty miles each way to church. That increases the service area for the very, very large full-service churches and raises the ceiling on their maximum size.

Will the Pendulum Swing Back?

As recently as 1955 most of the very large Protestant congregations in the United States carried one of four labels, Methodist, Baptist, Presbyterian, or Lutheran. It did not matter whether one was counting

Anglo or black churches, nearly all of the large ones were related to one of those four religious traditions. Another, but smaller, group of large congregations was affiliated with the Congregational Christian Church, The Christian Church (Disciples of Christ), The Reformed Church in America, The Evangelical and Reformed Church, The Episcopal Church, or one of the branches of the Church of God traditions. Today one of the two largest categories of large and growing full-service churches carries the label of Southern Baptist. Back in 1950 one Southern Baptist congregation out of every 273 reported a thousand or more members. By 1989 that ratio had changed to one out of every 128 reporting a thousand or more members.

The other big category of large and growing full-service churches today does not carry a denominational label. They usually are referred to as "independent" or "nondenominational" or "transdenominational."

Approximately 1 percent of all congregations affiliated with the Assemblies of God or with the Evangelical Free Church easily qualify as large and growing full-service churches.

In 1965 one out of every 216 Methodist congregations reported a thousand or more members. By 1988 that ratio had dropped to one out of every 285.

The big unknown is whether this trend will continue. Will the newer denominations and the independent churches account for an ever-growing proportion of the large full-service churches while the old mainline denominations report an ever-shrinking share?

Or will a new generation of entrepreneurial, visionary, skilled, energetic, enthusiastic, and persistent ministers come along and transform the face of the mainline denominations? Only the Lord knows the answer to that question. Here and there one can see signs of this beginning to happen in the Presbyterian Church (USA), the United Church of Christ, the Evangelical Lutheran Church in America, and in eight or ten conferences in The United Methodist Church in Texas, Oklahoma, Florida, Georgia, the Carolinas, and Indiana. Many of the old familiar brokerage names on Wall Street (Burnham, McKinnon, Bache, Hutton, Kuhn, Loeb, White, Weld, Becker, etc.) disappeared during the 1970–90 era.[17] Will the old familiar denominational names on large Protestant churches continue to disappear? Or will the old mainline Protestant denominations decide to make the large full-service program church a top priority in their planning for the twenty-first century? Will they be able to enlist the pastors required to make this happen? Will that goal receive the necessary support from denominational leaders?

The last of these yet-to-be-answered questions is the most speculative, the most subjective, and the most difficult to measure of any issue raised in this book.

Back during the peak of the big Sunday morning churches of the 1950s, it was common to find the senior minister of a large and numerically growing church who was theologically more liberal than the vast majority of the members. "I am more liberal than my preaching would lead you to believe," was the common observation of these pastors.

Today it is rare to find a very large and numerically growing full-service Protestant church on the North American continent in which the senior minister is theologically more liberal than the majority of the members. During the past four decades the people have moved to a more liberal position on issues of biblical interpretation, doctrine, prayer, divorce, sexuality, marriage, personal morality, and related subjects than were their counterparts of 1952. The clergy are scattered all across a broad spectrum of opinion, but the senior ministers of the very large and rapidly growing program churches often identify themselves as more conservative on these issues than are the people to whom they are preaching. This pattern is most highly visible in the very large churches reaching huge numbers of people born in the 1942–55 era.

In the year 2012, will the senior ministers of the very large Protestant churches be more liberal or more conservative than the generations born in the post-1968 era? Where will their preparatory years have been spent that will lead them to that position?

These and other questions plus many more that are yet to be articulated may be answered in a book about the full-service churches written by someone else in the year 2015. I wish I could have read it before writing this volume.

NOTES

Introduction

1. Five different perspectives on the megachurch are Jim Abrahamson, "In Search of the Effective Church," *Leadership,* Fall 1990, pp. 52-59, and the comments on that article, "The Responses of Effective Churches," *Leadership,* Winter 1991, pp. 89-91; Richard Lee Olson, "The Largest Congregations in the United States: An Empirical Study of Church Growth and Decline," unpublished Ph.D. dissertation (Evanston, Ill., Northwestern University, August 1988); Lyle E. Schaller, "Megachurch!" *Christianity Today,* March 5, 1990, pp. 20-24; Anthony B. Robinson, "Learning from Willow Creek," *The Christian Century,* January 23, 1991, pp. 68-70; and James Berkley, "The Marketing of a Boomer Church," *Christianity Today,* February 11, 1991, pp. 34-36.

2. See Lyle E. Schaller, "Lessons Across the Pacific," *Net Results,* May 1990, pp. 6-9.

3. For a definition of the homogeneous unit principle, see C. Peter Wagner, *Our Kind of People* (Atlanta: John Knox Press, 1979).

4. For the place of upward mobility in the early Christian churches, see Wayne A. Meeks, *The First Urban Christians* (New Haven: Yale University Press, 1983).

5. An introduction to Robert Buford, W. Fred Smith, and *The Leadership Network* can be found in Thomas A. Stewart, "Turning Around the Lord's Business," *Fortune,* September 25, 1989, p. 128.

6. For a superb analysis of the decline of denominationalism and the forces behind that trend, see Robert Wuthnow, *The Restructuring of American Religion* (Princeton, N.J.: Princeton University Press, 1988). For speculation on the emergence of new denominations, see Leo Parrott III and Robin J. Perrin, "The New Denominations!" *Christianity Today,* March 11, 1991, pp. 29-33.

1. The Changing Face of American Christianity

1. The statistics are from Edwin Scott Gaustad, *Historical Atlas of Religion in America* (New York: Harper & Row, 1982), pp. 4 and 48. Those who agree that both the changes of 1780–1820 and 1950–1990 qualify as "paradigm shifts" may want to read

an essay describing the change in the contemporary meaning of education in the United States. For this, see Chester E. Finn, Jr., "The Biggest Reform of All," *Phi Delta Kappan,* April 1990, pp. 585-92.

2. See Robert Wuthnow, *The Struggle for America's Soul* (Grand Rapids, Mich.: William B. Eerdmans, 1989).

3. See Dean R. Hoge et al. *Converts, Dropouts, Returnees* (New York: The Pilgrim Press, 1981).

4. See Martin E. Marty, Stuart E. Rosenberg, and Andrew M. Greeley, *What Do We Believe?* (New York: Meredith Press, 1968), pp. 287-306.

5. Andrew M. Greeley, *The Catholic Myth* (New York: Charles Scribner's Sons, 1990), pp. 4, 106-26.

6. Lyle E. Schaller, *It's a Different World!* (Nashville: Abingdon Press, 1987), pp. 86-92.

7. Jeffrey K. Hadden and Razelle Frankl, "Star Wars of a Different Kind: Reflections on the Politics of the Religion and Television Research Project," *Review of Religious Research,* December 1987, p. 103.

8. For an overview of the Church Growth Movement, see C. Peter Wagner, ed., *Church Growth: State of the Art* (Wheaton, Ill.: Tyndale House Publishers, 1986).

9. For an early prophetic word on the future of this type of congregation, see Ezra Earl Jones and Robert L. Wilson, *What's Ahead for Old First Church* (New York: Harper & Row, 1974). For a more recent word see Lyle E. Schaller, "Choices for Old First Church Downtown," *Choices for Churches* (Nashville: Abingdon Press, 1990), pp. 129-48.

10. Peter Drucker, *The New Realities* (New York: Harper & Row, 1989), p. 200.

11. A similar pattern in where people turn for help in the rest of American society is called "privatization." Hundreds of private organizations have been formed in recent decades to provide such services as fire fighting, employee training, protection of persons and property, the collection of garbage and trash, toll roads, education, data processing, and the imprisonment of persons convicted of a crime. These and other services once performed by governmental agencies are now being carried out by private contractors. See John D. Donahue, *The Privatization Decision* (New York: Basic Books, 1989). See also Myron Lieberman, *Privatization and Educational Choice* (New York: St. Martin's Press, 1989).

12. For two critiques of what types of persons are enrolling in theological seminaries today, see Jackson W. Carroll, "The State of the Art," *Christianity and Crisis,* April 3-17, 1989, pp. 106-16, and Paul Wilkes, "The Hands That Would Shape Our Souls," *The Atlantic,* December 1990, pp. 59-88.

13. The Leadership Network, in Tyler, Texas, has been a leader in encouraging the emergence of the teaching church, but many of today's best-known teaching churches predate the creation of The Leadership Network. Several Presbyterian (PCUSA) congregations accepted the teaching role back in the 1970s.

14. James P. Wind, "Congregational Studies: The Unexplored Territory," *Progressions,* January 1991, p. 21.

2. From Sunday Morning to Seven Days a Week

1. This and other styles of ministry are described in Lyle E. Schaller, *Choices for Churches* (Nashville: Abingdon Press, 1990), pp. 19-56.

2. Suggestions for the criteria in selecting a long-range planning committee and issues to

be addressed by such an ad hoc group can be found in Lyle E. Schaller, *Create Your Own Future!* (Nashville: Abingdon Press, 1991).

3. An exceptionally frank and lucid case study of the conflict between two groups of members with mutually incompatible goals can be found in Barry Johnson, "By Faith . . . Together!" in Robert L. Burt, ed., *Good News in Growing Churches* (New York: The Pilgrim Press, 1990), pp. 64-87. This readable volume is filled with case studies of churches that chose to create a new tomorrow rather than seek to perpetuate yesterday.

4. Peter F. Drucker, "The Non-Profits' Quiet Revolution," *The Wall Street Journal*, September 8, 1988.

5. Constant H. Jacquet, Jr., ed., *Yearbook of American and Canadian Churches, 1990* (Nashville: Abingdon Press, 1990), p. 259.

6. David W. Breneman, "Are We Losing Our Liberal Arts Colleges?" *The College Board Review*, Summer 1990, pp. 16-21.

7. Peter F. Drucker has described this same basic pattern in what he identifies as the emergence of "pastoral" churches. *The New Realities* (New York: Harper & Row, 1989), pp. 200-202.

8. In the early years secular organizations were far more responsive to this agenda than were the churches. For a popular discussion of self-help groups, but which oversimplifies the trend, see "Unite and Conquer," *Newsweek*, February 5, 1990, pp. 50-55. For the impact on book publishing, see Margaret Jones, "The Rage for Recovery," *Publishers Weekly*, November 23, 1990, pp. 16-24.

3. Why So Large?

1. An excellent brief on behalf of the innovative entrepreneur is Peter Drucker, *Innovation and Entrepreneurship* (New York: Harper & Row, 1985).

2. For a discussion of the personality cult issue, see Lyle E. Schaller, "Is Pastoral Ministry a Personality Cult?" *The Clergy Journal*, February 1987, pp. 31-32.

3. For a discussion of some of the differences between the "first-person church" and the "second-person church," see Lyle E. Schaller, *Looking in the Mirror* (Nashville: Abingdon Press, 1984), pp. 73-88.

4. George Plagenz, "Pulpit Must Be Good Theater," *The Pueblo* [Colorado] *Chieftain*, August 20, 1988.

5. While she is reflecting on her own faith journey, not on the emergence of the large program churches, McFague's provocative essay also offers a context for understanding other contemporary changes. See Sallie McFague, "An Earthly Theological Agenda," *The Christian Century*, January 2-9, 1991, pp. 12-15. A parallel statement, from a different perspective, on the redefinition of the liberal agenda in the large research university is offered by Harvey C. Mansfield, Jr., "The State of Harvard," *The Public Interest*, Fall 1990, pp. 113-23.

6. For an account on theological stance in one denomination, see Robert Wuthnow, *The Struggle for America's Soul* (Grand Rapids, Mich.: Eerdmans, 1989), pp. 68-96. See also James Davison Hunter, *Evangelicalism: The Coming Generation* (Chicago: University of Chicago Press, 1987).

7. For one example of direct mail inviting people to enroll in the Vacation Bible School, see Lyle E. Schaller, *44 Ways to Expand the Teaching Ministry of Your Church* (Nashville:

Abingdon Press, 1992). For a more extensive treatment of this subject, see Walter Mueller, *Direct Mail Ministry* (Nashville: Abingdon Press, 1989).

8. For an excellent discussion of the changing definitions of community, see Thomas Bender, *Community and Social Change in America* (New Brunswick, N.J.: Rutgers University Press, 1978).

9. For a superb statement on the importance of structure, see Francis A. J. Ianni, *The Search for Structure: A Report on American Youth Today* (New York: The Free Press, 1989).

10. For suggestions on bringing newcomers into the fellowship, see Lyle E. Schaller, *Assimilating New Members* (Nashville: Abingdon Press, 1978).

11. See Andrew Greeley, *The Catholic Myth* (New York: Charles Scribner's Sons, 1990).

12. Theodore Levitt, *Innovation in Marketing* (New York: McGraw-Hill Book Co., 1962).

13. For a brief statement on this, see Peter Drucker, *The New Realities* (New York: Harper & Row, 1989), pp. 200-202.

14. See Neil Postman, *Amusing Ourselves to Death* (New York: Penguin Books, 1985), pp. 30-63.

15. For a relevant discussion of how choice is transforming the marketplace, see Regis McKenna, "Marketing Is Everything," *The Harvard Business Review* (January–February 1991): 65-79.

16. An excellent case study of expanding the entry points in a large Presbyterian congregation is Thomas C. Albaum, "Double Doors for Singles Ministry," *Leadership,* Winter 1991, pp. 84-88.

4. Staffing the Full-Service Church

1. Although this is not the principal theme of the book, a description of the gap between the leaders with a liberal ideology and the lower middle-class culture of the working class can be found in Christopher Lasch, *The True and Only Heaven* (New York: W. W. Norton & Company, 1991). An exceptionally good book on younger generations of Americans is Tex Sample, *U.S. Lifestyles and Mainline Churches* (Louisville: Westminster/John Knox Press, 1990).

2. A superb training program for volunteers in a caring ministry has been created by Stephen Ministries, 1325 Boland, St.Louis, MO 63117. (Tel. 314-645-5511.)

3. For a longer discussion of the role of the ministry of music and the staffing of it, see Lyle E. Schaller, *The Senior Minister* (Nashville: Abingdon Press, 1988), pp. 100-122.

4. An excellent introduction to the Myers-Briggs Type Indicator and its application is Roy M. Oswald and Otto Kroeger, *Personality Type and Religious Leadership* (Washington, D.C.: The Alban Institute, 1988).

5. A superb analogy for the role of the senior minister is the wagon master who led the wagon trains across the great plains and mountains in the nineteenth century. The wagon master had two basic responsibilities: (1) to keep that wagon train heading west and (2) to maintain a reasonable degree of harmony among the members of the group. See J. S. Ninomiya, "Wagon Masters and Lesser Managers," *The Harvard Business Review* (March/April 1988): 84-90.

6. A wonderful statement of the distinction between a manager and a leader is offered by Warren Bennis and Burt Nanus, *Leaders: The Strategies for Taking Charge* (New

York: Harper & Row, 1985). "Managers are people who do things right and leaders are people who do the right thing" (p. 21). Those who are concerned about the hierarchical structure so often found in large congregations may be comforted by reading Elliott Jacques, "In Praise of Hierarchy," *Harvard Business Review* (January/February 1990): 127-33.

7. See Carl E. Larson and Frank M. J. LaFasto, *Teamwork: What Must Go Right/What Can Go Wrong* (Newbury Park, Calif.: Sage Publications, 1989). For alternative models of staff relationships, see Schaller, *The Senior Minister,* pp. 42-99.

5. Who Runs That Big Church?

1. For a more extensive discussion of the values of ad hoc committees, see Lyle E. Schaller, *Getting Things Done* (Nashville: Abingdon Press, 1986), chaps. 6 and 7. See also Lyle E. Schaller, *Create Your Own Future!* (Nashville: Abingdon Press, 1991), pp. 17-57.

2. A provocative insight on why participatory democracy has turned out to be a powerful tool for perpetuating the status quo is offered by Clark Kerr, *The Uses of the University,* 3rd ed. (Cambridge, Mass.: Harvard University Press, 1982), p. 177.

3. A frank, revealing, and lucid case study of congregational polity is provided by Barry L. Johnson, "By Faith . . . Together" in Robert L. Burt, ed., *Good News in Growing Churches* (New York: Pilgrim Press, 1990), pp. 64-87.

4. See Schaller, *Create Your Own Future!,* pp. 41-45.

5. John Stuart Mill, *On Liberty and Considerations on Representative Government* (Oxford: Blackwell, 1948), p. 161.

6. See John P. Witherspoon, "The Bureaucracy as Representatives," *Representation,* eds. J. Roland Pennock and John W. Chapman (New York: Atherton Press, 1968), pp. 233-39.

7. A useful book on the role of boards in voluntary associations and public agencies is John Carver, *Boards That Make a Difference* (San Francisco: Jossey-Bass Publishers, 1990). Carver projects more optimistic expectations of the board as initiating leaders than I do.

8. For alternative ways of responding to passivity, see Lyle E. Schaller, *Activating the Passive Church* (Nashville: Abingdon Press, 1981).

6. Continuity and Succession

1. A useful book for congregations faced with finding a successor to the senior minister is Thomas North Gilmore, *Making a Leadership Change* (San Francisco: Jossey-Bass Publishers, 1988). See also Lyle E. Schaller, "Picking a New Pastor," *The Pastor and the People,* rev. ed. (Nashville: Abingdon Press, 1986), pp. 19-32.

7. Clouds and Questions

1. The statistics on retail grocery sales are taken from U.S. Bureau of the Census, *Statistical Abstract of the United States: 1990* (Washington, D.C.: U.S. Government Printing Office, 1990), p. 774.

2. Recent years have brought a flood of articles in the secular press on the proliferation of the very large program churches. For example, see "And the Children Lead Them," *Newsweek,* December 17, 1990; Cathleen Ferraro, "Churches Turning to Marketing to

Increase Size of Their Flocks," *Investors Daily*, February 7, 1991; Thomas A. Stewart, "Turning the Lord's Business Around," *Fortune*, September 25, 1989. Barbara Dolan, "Full House at Willow Creek," *Time*, March 6, 1987, p. 69; Gustav Niebuhr, "Megachurches Strive to Be All Things to All Parishioners," *Wall Street Journal*, May 13, 1991, p. 1; Richard N. Ostling, "Superchurches and How They Grew," *Time*, August 5, 1991, pp. 62-63. The two common themes of these articles are marketing and the competition in reaching the generations born after World War II.

3. A delightful account of how a mortgage can subvert goals was written by Charles Lee Wilson and can be found in Lyle E. Schaller, *Hey, That's Our Church!* (Nashville: Abingdon Press, 1975), p. 105.

4. An introduction to the problem of legal restrictions on the use of land for religious purposes can be found in Scott Daniel Godschall, "Land Use Regulation and the Free Exercise Clause," *Columbia Law Review* 84, 6 (October 1984): 1562-89.

5. The evolution of the concept of the parish nurse can be found in Phyllis Ann Solari-Twadell, Anne Marie Djupe, and Mary Ann McDermott, *Parish Nursing: The Developing Practice*. Suggestions on how to initiate the program can be found in Granger E. Westberg and Jill Westberg McNamara, *The Parish Nurse*. Both books are published by the National Parish Nurse Resource Center, Parkside Center, 1876 Dempster St., Park Ridge, Illinois 60068. See also Lawrence E. Holst, "The Parish Nurse," *Chronicle of Pastoral Care* (Spring/Summer 1987): 13-17.

6. Jill Westberg McNamara, *The Health Cabinet* (Park Ridge, Ill.: Parish Nurse Resource Center, 1981).

7. I am indebted to James S. Coleman and Thomas Hoffer, *Public and Private High Schools* (New York: Basic Books, Inc., 1987) for several of the concepts discussed here.

8. An excellent history of the origins of private Christian schools in the United States is Otto F. Kraushaar, *American Nonpublic Schools* (Baltimore: The Johns Hopkins University Press, 1972), pp. 3-88.

9. This account of Atkinson's life and work is drawn from David Tyack and Elizabeth Hansot, *Managers of Virtue* (New York: Basic Books, Inc., 1982).

10. Ibid., pp. 78-80.

11. Coleman and Hoffer, *Public and Private High Schools*, pp. 3-10.

12. Lloyd Jorgenson, *The Founding of Public Education in Wisconsin* (Madison: State Historical Society of Wisconsin, 1956), p. 145.

13. See Lyle E. Schaller, "The Role of Private Christian Schools," *The MPL Journal* 5, 1 (1984). See also Patricia Lines, "The New Private Schools and Their Historic Purpose," *Phi Delta Kappan* (January 1986): 373-79.

14. The literature on the condition of the public schools is voluminous. Especially useful books are Coleman and Hoffer, *Public and Private High Schools*; William Glasser, *The Quality School* (New York: Harper & Row, 1990); Jeannie Oakes, *Keeping Track* (New Haven: Yale University Press, 1985); Sharon L. Kagan and Edward F. Zigler, eds., *Early Schooling: The National Debate* (New Haven: Yale University Press, 1987); John E. Chubb and Terry M. Moe, *Politics, Markets, and America's Schools* (Washington: The Brookings Institution, 1990); Lawrence A. Cremin, *Popular Education and Its Discontents* (New York: Harper & Row, 1989); Myron Lieberman, *Public School Choice: Current Issues and Future Prospects* (Lancaster, Pa.: Technomic Publishers, 1990).

15. A provocative defense of homeschooling by a father who teaches English in a public high school is David Guterson, "When Schools Fail Children," *Harper's Magazine,* November 1990, pp. 58-64.

16. *Debates on Education Issues,* the successor to *Character* and *Character II* is a newsletter that "aims to broaden the intellectual options researched and debated about education and youth issues." Write to: Professor Edward A. Wynne, College of Education, The University of Illinois at Chicago, Box 4348, Chicago, Illinois 60680 for details. A fascinating journalistic book on this subject is Richard Louv, *Children's Future* (Boston: Houghton Mifflin, 1990).

17. William Power, "Name-Dropping on Wall Street No Longer What It Used to Be," *The Wall Street Journal,* February 22, 1991.